Alberta
Originals

Alberta Originals

STORIES OF ALBERTANS WHO MADE A DIFFERENCE

Brian Brennan

FIFTH
HOUSE

Cover and interior design by John Luckhurst / GDL
Front cover photograph by Daryl Benson / Masterfile

The publisher gratefully acknowledges the support of The Canada Council for the
Arts and the Department of Canadian Heritage. We acknowledge the financial sup-
port of the Government of Canada through the Book Publishing Industry
Development Program for our publishing activities.

Printed in Canada.

01 02 03 04 05/ 5 4 3 2 1

National Library of Canada Cataloguing in Publication Data

Includes index.
  ISBN 1-894004-76-0

  1. Alberta—Biography. I. Title.
  FC3655.B725 2001   920.07123   C2001-911272-6
  F1075.8.B725 2001

Fifth House Ltd.
A Fitzhenry & Whiteside Company
1511-1800 4 St. SW
Calgary, Alberta, Canada
T2S 2S5

1-800-387-9776
www.fitzhenry.ca

To Zelda and Nicole

Contents

Introduction

Ralph Klein likely wouldn't appreciate the comparison, but I see some striking similarities between the current Alberta premier and his predecessor of the Great Depression, William "Bible Bill" Aberhart.

Both worked in broadcasting before entering politics. Klein was a radio and television reporter with CFCN in Calgary when he ran successfully for mayor in 1980. Aberhart was the host of CFCN Radio's popular *Back to the Bible Hour* when he became Alberta's first Social Credit premier in 1935. And, by remarkable coincidence, both took their budgetary cues from eccentric foreign theorists named Douglas. Klein's economic visionary was Sir Roger Douglas, a politician from New Zealand who coined the slogan, "Don't blink." Aberhart's fiscal hero was Major Clifford Douglas, a Scottish electrical engineer whose catch phrase was "Poverty in the midst of plenty."

I didn't intend initially to include Aberhart when I started choosing Albertans for this book. He was already the subject of at least three full-length biographies, and I felt I would have little to add to what was already written about the man. However, his name kept cropping up regularly in stories I was writing about other Albertans, so I eventually decided that the ghost should assume bodily form and substance. He looms large in Alberta myth. As biographers Christina McCall and Stephen Clarkson said about Pierre Elliott Trudeau, "He haunts us still."

Though he died the year I was born, 1943, Aberhart has been haunting me, it seems, ever since I came to Canada from Ireland in 1966 and settled first in Vancouver. The province of British Columbia had been governed in the name of Social Credit for fourteen years before I arrived, and the Social Credit name was synonymous with "Bible Bill" Aberhart. Who was this quixotic preacher from the Prairies who spawned a political movement that spread from Alberta to British Columbia and to the House of Commons? That's the question that finally led to my including Aberhart in this volume of biographical profiles.

To me, Aberhart was and remains an enigma. Like Ralph Klein today, he always seemed more comfortable preaching borrowed economic ideas into a microphone than trying to explain the logic behind them when the tough questions were asked. What made Aberhart tick? Probing an enigma poses an irresistible challenge for a biographer.

Choosing the other Albertans for this book resulted from the same non-scientific, idiosyncratic, and you might say, entirely personal process. Some of them, like Aberhart and his successor Ernest Manning, were already well known. But to me and I'm sure to others of my generation, they were known in name only. When I came to Alberta in 1974, Manning had been gone from provincial politics for six years. His name still resonated in discussions about the Socred government that Peter Lougheed's Conservatives had toppled in 1971. However, the record of Manning's achievement was known only to political science students and to those who were around in the 1940s and 1950s to witness Manning leading Alberta from the lingering devastation of the Great Depression to the unparalleled prosperity of the post-war oil boom.

And who were the "Famous Five" and the "Big Four"? Again, we are dealing here with people whose names are well known in this province but only, perhaps, for the single achievements that brought them lasting fame and a place in the history books. The Famous Five lobbied for the constitutional change that resulted in Canadian women becoming eligible for Senate appointments. The Big Four put up the money for the first Calgary Stampede. What else do we know about them? Do we even know their individual names? I certainly didn't until I started writing about them for this book. I might have been able to name Nellie McClung and Pat Burns, but I would not have known about Louise McKinney or Archie McLean.

Researching the stories of the Famous Five and the Big Four has allowed me to learn about the lives of some renowned individuals who contributed something important to the building of this province. Because their personal stories have been overshadowed by their public achievements, as people they fall into the same little-known category as the more obscure individuals included in this book.

What made them tick? That's the question that drives all the stories here. In many instances, I haven't been able to find the answers because for the most part I have relied on second-hand sources, i.e., previously published accounts, for my information, and sometimes the information simply isn't there. For all the words that have been written about Aberhart, for example, none begins to explain why he embraced a secular political philosophy so entirely opposed to his fundamentalist belief in the divine ordering of life's affairs. But finding answers is never the point. Asking the right questions is.

So how did I choose the subjects for this book? In a word, randomly, but that's not to say indiscriminately. I looked for people who either helped build the social, economic, cultural, or political foundations of this province or who added to what had already been built.

In many instances, I picked individuals who lived according to the philosophy of an Alberta philanthropist who once said that community service was rent due for space occupied. These include such altruistic individuals as the Edmonton arts and education benefactor Francis Winspear, Banff's museum founder Catharine Robb Whyte, and Calgary businessmen Max Bell and Ralph Scurfield who gave millions back to their community. In other instances, I picked people who enlivened the history of this province with their colourful personalities. These include the likes of the adventurer Morris "Two-Gun" Cohen; the controversial Edmonton mayor, William Hawrelak; Banff's man about the mountains, Bruno Engler; and the flamboyant film producer, Les Kimber.

Albertans who broke new ground are prominently featured throughout the book. These include the ballet pioneer, Ruth Carse; the black lawyer, Violet King Henry; the Native broadcaster, Eugene Steinhauer; the midwifery advocate, Sandra Botting; the oil patch explorer, Bill Herron; and the developmental education pioneer, Christine Meikle; as well as some of the more traditional kinds of pioneers such as the ranchers, Henry Frank Lawrence and Monica Hopkins; the missionary, Martin Holdom; and the father of Calgary's Chinatown, Ho Lem. I have also included a few Albertans who reached for the top and made it to the winner's podium: cow-boy king, Herman Linder; sportswoman, Pearl Borgal; and jockey, Jimmy Fitzsimmons.

There was no grand plan attached to the process of choosing Albertans for this book, no schematic ordering of subjects along demographic lines. I simply went from story to story as I was com-posing the text and hoped—like Robert Fitzpatrick, the man who booked the entertainment acts for the arts festival at the 1984 Los Angeles Summer Olympics—that if the stories appealed to me, they would appeal to you the reader.

So this book, like my first Fifth House publication, *Building a Province: 60 Alberta Lives*, is neither definitive nor comprehensive, but it is, I suggest, representative. It offers a valid sampling of the var-ious people who spent time in Alberta during its first century and left their imprints either here or in other places. The thread that connects them all is that they were originals. They marched to the beat of their own drum corps and created a rhythm that was truly special, truly unique, truly Albertan.

As always, I have many people to thank for helping bring this book to fruition. Writing for publication is a solitary and often lonely endeavour and it cannot happen without a good support system. Mine includes: Charlene Dobmeier, the publisher of Fifth House, who grants me the freedom to write stories about Albertans I find interesting; Judy Hamill, the host of CBC Radio's *Daybreak Alberta*, who invites me to talk on the air about Alberta lives well lived; Don Smith, the University of Calgary history professor, whose enthusias-tic support for my journalistic forays into historical matters is truly gratifying and humbling; my gregarious Calgary chapter colleagues in the Periodical Writers Association of Canada, who give me terrific suggestions and advice (they were the ones who urged me to write about Aberhart); and Zelda Brennan, my beloved life's partner and soul-mate, whose love, understanding, and patience always sustain me.

Brian Brennan
Calgary, May 2001

The Famous Five

Social reformers and crusaders
for women's rights

Henrietta Muir Edwards 1849–1931

Louise McKinney 1868–1931

Emily Murphy 1868–1933

Irene Parlby 1868–1965

Nellie McClung 1873–1951

Beyond building a province, the Famous Five helped build a nation. They won the right to have Canadian women legally recognized as "persons" and thus eligible to hold public positions including Senate appointments. Because of that notable achievement, the Famous Five rank well above all others as Alberta's most significant contributors to the advancement of women in Canadian public life during the twentieth century.

Their journey toward equality began with Emily Murphy, a self-taught legal expert from Cookstown, Ontario, who wrote freelance articles under the pen name "Janey Canuck" and worked for a variety of causes in the interests of women and children. In 1916, Murphy was appointed to the bench in Edmonton and so became the first woman magistrate in the British Empire.

Quest for Equality Begins

On her first day in court, Judge Murphy faced a hostile defence lawyer, Eardley Jackson, who asserted that as a woman she had no status under British law. "You're not even a person," objected Jackson. "You have no right to be holding court." He based his claim on a decision rendered in 1876 by an English court stating, "Women are persons in matters of pains and penalties, but are not persons in matters of rights and privileges." "Since the office of magistrate is a

5

privilege," argued Jackson, "the current magistrate sits illegally. No decision coming from her court may bind anyone."

Jackson clearly didn't realize it at the time, but he had unwittingly given Murphy another cause on which to work. She politely noted his objection, continued with her sentencing, and then spent the next dozen years leading a determined fight to have Canadian women legally recognized as "persons" for the purpose of holding public office.

In Calgary, magistrate Alice Jamieson faced a similar challenge. When she took her place on the bench in late 1916, shortly after Murphy's appointment, male lawyers, police, and fellow judges contested her right as a female and as a "non-person" to make binding judicial decisions. She brought the matter to the Alberta Supreme Court, which ruled in 1917 that there was "no legal disqualification for holding public office in the government of this country on the basis of sex." So, in Alberta at least, Murphy and Jamieson were viewed as "persons."

In Ottawa it was a different story. The federal government, operating under the British North American Act, insisted that women were not persons "in matters of rights and privileges." This did not sit well with Emily Murphy. She was supported by the 450,000-member National Council of Women and entertained ambitions of becoming Canada's first female senator.

In 1927, Murphy discovered a little-known section of the Supreme Court Act that allowed five individuals to petition the government for clarification of any part of the British North America Act. She invited four friends—Louise McKinney, Nellie McClung, Henrietta Muir Edwards, and Irene Parlby—to add their signatures to a letter addressed to the Governor General asking that the Supreme Court rule on two constitutional questions: "1. Is power vested in the Governor-General in Council of Canada, or the Parliament of Canada, or either of them, to appoint a female to the Senate of Canada? 2. Is it constitutionally possible for the Parliament of Canada under the provisions of the British North America Act, or otherwise, to make provision for the appointment of a female to the Senate of Canada."

Separately Strong

The five women, while coming from different backgrounds, had much in common. All spent years fighting for the same political rights as men, and all subscribed to an English-Canadian imperialist vision, commonly held in the 1920s, of a strong Canada playing an active and dynamic role in the British Empire. Seasoned militants, the five women were active politically both inside and outside the Alberta legislature and were also well known as activists in the temperance, suffragette, and women's movements.

Murphy, born into the prosperous Ferguson family of Cookstown, Ontario, came west with her husband and two daughters when she was thirty-five. She initially settled in Swan River, Manitoba, and then, in 1907, moved to Edmonton where she combined family life with freelance writing for Canadian newspapers and magazines. Married to an Anglican missionary, Arthur Murphy, who left the ministry to start a business in timber and real estate, she adopted the pen name "Janey Canuck" while en route to England by boat after she heard a British woman making disparaging remarks about "Canucks." Murphy decided mischievously that she would assume the name as a matter of national pride. When her first book, *Impressions of Janey Canuck Abroad,* won laudatory reviews from the British critics, she felt vindicated.

Along with her writing and her family life, Murphy was active in social causes for women. When she discovered there were no property laws on the books that would protect a wife's interest in the family home—or even give her the right to know of transactions involving her home Murphy resolved to press for provincial legislation that would provide such protection. Henrietta Muir Edwards, a china painter and women's rights activist from Fort Macleod, supported her in this initiative. Edwards seemed to know almost everything there was to know about laws as they related to women and children.

Edwards acquired her legal expertise while serving as Convener of Laws for the National Council of Women in Canada, an organization she co-founded in Ottawa in 1893. Born in 1849, to the wealthy Muir family in Montreal, Henrietta embraced evangelical Christianity as a young girl and spent the rest of her life practising what was preached, doing "good works" on behalf of others. She established for young working women in downtown Montreal a residence and reading room that was a forerunner of the Young Women's Christian Association, and she published a magazine, *Women's Work in Canada,* which was Canada's first publication aimed exclusively at women. She financed her social work through her china painting rather than take money from her wealthy family.

In 1876, Henrietta married physician Oliver Edwards. They lived in what is now Saskatchewan for seven years and raised three children. They moved back to Montreal in 1890, and then lived in Ottawa for a few years. Henrietta worked with Lady Aberdeen, wife of the Governor General, to help establish both the Victorian Order of Nurses and the National Council of Women (NCW), an umbrella organization for all the women's groups in Canada. In 1903, the Edwards family moved west again, this time to the Blood Reserve near Fort Macleod, Alberta. Oliver served as resident doctor on the reserve while Henrietta continued with her NCW work, which followed her wherever she lived. Because Oliver was a poor provider, Henrietta was often in dire straits, trying to finance her unpaid research and social work with her china painting. Her most notable achievement in that regard was a set of china that she painted for the Canadian Art Exhibit at the 1893 World's Fair in Chicago.

As national Convener of Laws for the NCW, Edwards became quite an expert in the field of Canadian law concerning women and children. Lawyers and judges began to ask her for advice after she published one government handbook on the legal status of women in Canada and another handbook relating to Alberta laws.

Edwards did her research work in the law library at Edmonton's legislative buildings, and that's where she first met Emily Murphy, who was researching some legal matters of her own. Together they lobbied the provincial government for a law protecting the property rights of married women.

In 1911, the Alberta government enacted the Married Women's Protective Act. It wasn't as strong as Murphy and Edwards would have liked, but it was a start in that it guaranteed a wife one-third of her husband's estate upon his death, no matter what his will said. Murphy and Edwards continued to press for improvements to the legislation until the government brought in two amending bills, the Married Women's Home Protection Act of 1915 and the Dower Act of 1916. The first gave a wife the right to file an official request to a court to prevent the sale or mortgage of her home without her permission. The second gave a wife the right to live until death on the "homestead," i.e., the property she occupied during her marriage. It also required that the wife's written consent be granted before the property could be sold or otherwise disposed of.

During this same period, in the early years of the First World War, Murphy and Edwards became involved in the fight to gain Albertan women the vote. Spearheading this fight, for both the women's vote and for prohibition, were the black-stockinged members of the Women's Christian Temperance Union (WCTU), whose desire to rid the frontier of drinking, gambling, and prostitution led to them supporting causes aimed at civilizing, humanizing, and christianizing the Canadian West. Prominent among them was Louise McKinney, a WCTU organizer from Claresholm.

McKinney, born Louise Crummy in 1868, learned early in life that women were not born equal to men. A church-going Methodist from Frankville, Ontario, she abandoned plans to become a physician when her father told her nobody would ever want to visit a female doctor. Instead she became a teacher and temperance advocate. "I will never falter until this land is freed from the bonds of the distiller, brewer, and government company," she pledged.

In 1893, at age twenty-five, Louise moved to North Dakota to teach and to do some organizing for the WCTU. She met and married James McKinney, a Methodist minister who shared her desire to rid the world of alcohol. They named their son Willard after Frances Willard, the founder of the WCTU in the United States.

The McKinneys moved up to Claresholm, Alberta, in 1903. James built a church there, and Louise continued with her WCTU organizing activities. Between 1903 and 1912, she organized forty-three WCTU chapters in Alberta and Saskatchewan.

Her involvement in the fight for women's suffrage was a natural extension of her work with the WCTU. McKinney believed that if women received the vote, alcohol would be outlawed. She also saw a link between drinking and family violence, and gambling.

Elimination of alcohol would solve a lot of social problems, she thought.

McKinney's efforts began to be rewarded in 1915 when Alberta introduced prohibition. Later that year, Premier Arthur L. Sifton, responding to a fifty-thousand-name petition from women's suffrage campaigners, announced that Albertan women could vote in the next provincial election. Inspired by the example of Nellie McClung in Manitoba, the Alberta suffragettes had spent four years fighting for the same political rights as men.

McClung had left Manitoba and was living in Edmonton when women in Manitoba received the vote in 1916, so she didn't get to join the victory parade in Winnipeg, but she did get to share the credit when Alberta women received the vote later that year.

A writer and temperance advocate, McClung was born in 1873 to the Mooney family of Chatsworth, Ontario. In 1880, the family moved to Manitoba where Nellie's father hoped to find land and opportunity for his six children. Nellie trained as a teacher, married insurance salesman Wes McClung, raised five children, then switched occupational gears and began writing fiction.

McClung's first novel, *Sowing Seeds in Danny*, sold so well after publication in 1908 that she decided to make a career in writing. While on the road promoting the novel, she discovered she had a gift for public speaking and that became part of her career as well. Through the WCTU and the Women's Political Equality League in Winnipeg, which she helped found, she advocated for prohibition and women's suffrage, called for improved working conditions for women in factories, and lobbied for more protective laws for women and children.

In 1914, Wes McClung was transferred to Edmonton with his insurance business, and Nellie brought along her causes and her passion. She was among the hundreds of women who descended on the provincial legislature in February 1915 and called upon Premier Sifton to give women the vote. Also there were Emily Murphy, Henrietta Muir Edwards, and judge Alice Jamieson from Calgary. "Mrs. McClung and Mrs. Murphy are very determined women," the premier later told the press.

Initial Victories

On 28 January 1916, Manitoba became the first province in Canada to grant women the vote. Saskatchewan followed a month later. Alberta's turn came on April 16. Murphy, McClung, and Jamieson celebrated by having their photograph taken at an Edmonton studio. "Being women," explained Jamieson, "we couldn't very well express our joy and satisfaction by going out and getting a bottle."

The provincial election of 1917 gave Alberta women their first opportunity to exercise their newly won franchise. It also gave them a first opportunity to run for elected office at the provincial level. Louise McKinney was one of those who ran, as an independent candidate in Claresholm, and she became the first woman to sit in a legislative body anywhere in the British Empire. However, it was just a technical first because Roberta MacAdams from Edmonton was elected the same year. MacAdams, however, didn't get to take her seat until she finished serving as a nursing sister with the armed forces overseas.

In 1921, McKinney ran for re-election, again as an independent because she had heard that organized political parties accepted funds from liquor companies. She wore the white ribbon of temperance as a badge of honour. However, public attitudes toward drinking were changing. The men who came home from the war were upset with the WCTU because it had opposed both tobacco and liquor for the servicemen. McKinney's opposition to drinking and smoking became her political downfall. She lost by forty-six votes to her United Farmers of Alberta (UFA) opponent. Two years later, prohibition was defeated in a provincial referendum. The WCTU never recovered from the setback.

Many considered McKinney's defeat a significant loss, but she had other fish to fry. Her life hinged on her religious faith, not on politics. After co-signing the Basis of Union that produced the United Church of Canada from a combination of Methodist, Congregationalist, and Presbyterian Churches, she began travelling across Canada as a lay preacher.

Nellie McClung entered provincial politics just as McKinney was leaving. She won as a Liberal candidate in Edmonton in 1921, and sat in loyal opposition to the ruling UFA party. Also elected that year,

11

as a UFA member, was Irene Parlby of Lacombe, provincial president of the United Farm Women of Alberta (UFWA).

Parlby, born to the aristocratic Marryat family in England and raised in India, had been living in Canada for twenty-two years when she ran for provincial office. She came to what is now Alberta at age twenty-eight to visit friends on a ranch near Alix, east of Lacombe. She met and married Walter Parlby, a scholar of Greek classics, also from England, and one of the first white settlers in the area. They set up housekeeping at Dartmoor Ranch, named after Walter's Devonshire homeland, and raised a son, Humphrey.

The Parlbys helped establish libraries, schools, roads, and other services in their community. Irene joined the Alix Country Women's Club, a social club that evolved into an auxiliary of the United Farmers of Alberta and eventually achieved autonomy as a branch of the United Farm Women of Alberta. In 1916, she was elected president of the UFWA.

Parlby, a reluctant politician at best, only agreed to run for provincial office in 1921 because she didn't expect that either the UFA or she would be elected. Both won handily at the polls. "I didn't know whether to laugh or cry," said Parlby. During her years in politics, she would always be torn between her civic responsibilities and her desire to retreat to her garden, her books, and what she called "my own chimney corner."

When Parlby arrived in Edmonton, the new premier, Herbert Greenfield, named her Minister Without Portfolio, and she thus became the first woman in Alberta to serve as a cabinet minister. The appointment virtually guaranteed that the reluctant politician would remain in politics for a while longer.

Although Nellie McClung sat with the Opposition across the floor, that didn't stop her from working with Parlby on laws relating to women and children. The issues were what mattered, not the dictates of party policy. One of the bills that Parlby sponsored, and which McClung supported, was the 1925 Minimum Wage for Women Act.

McClung moved with her family to Calgary in 1923 and commuted back and forth to Edmonton. She sought re-election as a Calgary candidate in 1926, but she lost by sixty votes. Parlby regained her seat in Lacombe, and returned to the cabinet as Minister Without Portfolio.

Strength in Numbers: The Famous Five

When the call came from Emily Murphy in 1927 to join her petition to the Supreme Court, McClung, Parlby, Edwards, and McKinney were ready to participate. After Ontario's Agnes Macphail was elected to the House of Commons in 1921, thus becoming the first Canadian woman to sit as an MP, admitting women to the Senate became once again a burning issue. The 1923 death of Alberta Liberal senator Amédée-Emmanuel Forget revived the Alberta women's militancy. They seized the opportunity and proposed that Emily Murphy be appointed to fill the vacant seat.

Murphy had been busy for the previous decade with her social activism, her writing, and her magistrate's work. As a magistrate, an experience she likened to "running a rapids without a guide," she brought justice tempered with mercy. "Magistrates should not be there to blister people but to help them," she said. To prove the point, she often invited young female defendants to the Murphy home for supper to talk about morals and their plans for the future.

Murphy published four books under the pen name of "Janey Canuck," all of them best-selling sketches of life in western Canada. Under her own name she wrote *The Black Candle*, a book about the evils of the drug trade. It led to federal laws governing narcotics that remained unchanged until the late 1960s. She also courted controversy by writing a series of magazine articles in favour of sexually sterilizing people considered "psychotic" or "mentally defective." Canada needed "human thoroughbreds" but was burdened with "lunatics," she wrote. "We protect the public against diseased and distempered cattle. We should similarly protect them against the offal of humanity."

Murphy was not alone in her pro-sterilization beliefs. Among the early Canadian supporters of eugenics—the pseudo-science of improving the human species through selective breeding—were the inventor, Alexander Graham Bell; physician, William Osler; and the pioneering socialist, Tommy Douglas. In Alberta, the eugenics movement was spearheaded by the WCTU and the UFWA who blamed

Canada's lax immigration policy for an influx of thousands of "criminal and mental degenerates." The UFWA declared that something had to be done because "democracy was never intended for degenerates" and called upon the province to pass a sterilization law that would prevent the emergence of social problems. The UFA government responded with the Sexual Sterilization Act of 1928, an act that remained on the books until 1972, long after such legislation had been discredited elsewhere.

It seems unthinkable today that women would have supported compulsory sexual sterilization to prevent people with perceived mental deficiencies from procreating. However, as Calgary historian Anne White has written, "The demand that they (Emily Murphy and others) possess a fully integrated liberal view according to our modern interpretation is unreasonable ... It is wrong to criticize the women for not meeting our standards today as our standards have developed out of the reforms they initiated."

The principal reform initiated by Murphy and her colleagues, pushing to have the Senate doors opened to women, got off to a rocky start. First, the wording of the petition was changed, without their knowledge or consent, to eliminate references to females being appointed to the Senate. Instead, the question posed to the Supreme Court was, "Does the word 'Persons' in Section 24 of the British North America Act, 1867, include female persons?" Section 24 stated "the Governor General shall from Time to Time ... summon qualified persons to the Senate." Properly qualified persons had to be at least thirty years old, hold property, be worth at least four thousand dollars, and live in the province for which they were appointed. Numerous women met the requirements. It remained to be seen if they were "persons."

Murphy was livid when she received a copy of the petition and saw that the wording had been changed. She wrote to the Deputy Justice Minister, W. Stuart Edwards, pointing out that the question referred to the Supreme Court was "not the one submitted by your petitioners either in word or in meaning and is, in consequence, a matter of amazement and perturbation to us." Edwards replied that the only power allowing admission into the Senate was conferred by the BNA Act upon the Governor General, and it was evident that the exercise of that power rested on the interpretation of the word "persons" in Section 24. Therefore, the only relevant question was to determine if this word included women.

On 24 April 1928, the Supreme Court of Canada rendered its decision and declared that women were not persons. Despite that decision, Justice Minister Ernest Lapointe declared that women *did* have a legal right to sit in the Senate, and that eventually measures would be taken to amend the BNA Act accordingly. However, Emily Murphy was not going to wait around for such eventuality. Undaunted, she resolved to appeal to the Judicial Committee of the Privy Council in London, England, which was, at that time, the final court of appeal for Canadians. "Nothing can prevent our winning," she wrote to her four co-appellants.

The Privy Council hearing on the "Persons Case," as it was dubbed in the press, was set for 18 July 1929, and continued on 23 and 25 July. Newspapers on both sides of the Atlantic took an active interest in the case, and referred to the women in front-page headlines as the "Alberta Five" or the "Famous Five." The case became known in legal annals as *Edwards versus the Attorney General of Canada,* because the names of the five appellants were listed in alphabetical order.

Women Are Persons

On 18 October 1929, the Privy Council ruled in favour of women, declaring that they were indeed persons and therefore eligible to sit in the Senate of Canada. "The exclusion of women from all public offices is a relic of days more barbarous than ours," wrote the British judges. "The word 'persons' may include members of both sexes." The Famous Five celebrated their victory with a tea party at the Palliser Hotel in Calgary.

Four months later, in February 1930, Prime Minister Mackenzie King seized the opportunity to be the first government leader to allow women into the Senate, but he didn't appoint Murphy, or any other member of the Famous Five. Instead, the honour went to Cairine Wilson, a Montreal philanthropist and Liberal party supporter. King told a cabinet colleague that Murphy was "a little too masculine and perhaps a bit too flamboyant."

Murphy hoped her call to the Senate might come at a later date, but it never did. She went home to Edmonton disappointed, and in 1933, at age sixty-five, she died there, some said, of a broken heart. The official medical reason was heart failure brought on by diabetes. The City of Edmonton dedicated a riverside park in her memory.

None of the Famous Five ever got to hold the position for which they had fought so hard. In fact, Alberta didn't get its first female senator until 1979, when Prime Minister Joe Clark appointed Martha Bielish from Warspite.

McKinney and Edwards died two years after the landmark Privy Council decision that declared women as persons. McKinney died in June 1931 shortly after chairing a national WCTU conference in Toronto. Edwards died the following November at age eighty-two.

McClung lived in Calgary until 1932, when she and Wes retired to Victoria. True to form, she became the first woman on the CBC's Board of Governors, and she wrote two biographies, *Clearing in the West* and *My Own Story*. All told, she wrote a total of sixteen books. She died in 1951 at age seventy-eight. During the 1970s, the Calgary Status of Women Action committee successfully petitioned the Alberta government to designate her Calgary house a provincial historic site.

Parlby continued to serve her Lacombe constituency until 1935, when, at age sixty-seven, she finally retired from politics. She left the year the UFA yielded power to William Aberhart's Social Credit party, retired to her quiet country home in Alix, and spent the next thirty years tending her garden and watching her grandchildren grow up. She died in 1965 at age ninety-seven, the last of the Famous Five to die.

For close to sixty years, the only memorial jointly commemorating the Famous Five as a group was a bronze plaque installed in 1938 at the entrance to the Senate chamber in Ottawa by the Calgary branch of the Canadian Federation of Business and Professional Women. Then, starting in 1996, there was a flurry of commemorative activity.

On 18 October 1996, the sixty-seventh anniversary of the historic Persons Case decision, a newly launched Famous Five Foundation held its inaugural meeting at Calgary's Palliser Hotel. An aim of the foundation was to create a permanent memorial for the Famous Five in the province in which they had launched their successful petition. Three years later, on the seventieth anniversary, the Famous Five were honoured with the unveiling on Calgary's Olympic Plaza of *Women are Persons!*, a commemorative, larger-than-life tableau of bronze statues by artist Barbara Paterson. Calgary author Nancy Millar published a book, *The Famous Five: Emily Murphy and the Case of the Missing Persons*, and the federal government issued a commemorative stamp.

On 18 October 2000, the seventy-first anniversary, a second edition of the Paterson tableau of statues was installed on Parliament Hill in Ottawa as a permanent memorial. Later that year, the Bank of Canada issued a new fifty dollar bill, honouring both the Famous Five and Thérèse Casgrain, who led the campaign for women's suffrage in Quebec. Together, these women helped build Canada. Now it falls to their successors to build on their success.

Frank Oliver

Newspaperman and politician

1853–1933

For some Edmontonians, Frank Oliver is considered the greatest Albertan of the twentieth century. He used his political influence to ensure that Edmonton, not Calgary, would become the provincial capital even though the southern city was twice as big in the early 1900s and the transcontinental railway ran through it.

However, that achievement might not make Oliver a hero in the eyes of other Albertans, particularly Calgarians. Also going against him is the fact that Oliver had what today would be regarded as major personality flaws. He was, for better and worse, a man of his time and place. He scorned Natives and other non-whites, and pursued legislative policies that were racist and discriminatory.

Yet despite all this, it is probably fair to say that Oliver made some important contributions to the early development of his adopted home in the Canadian Northwest, especially during the years leading up to provincehood. Among them was his establishment of the first newspaper in what is now Alberta, his creation of the territory's first public school system, and his formation of Canada's first national park in the Banff area.

Oliver was committed to the future of his adopted home from the moment in October 1876 when he pitched his tent on the banks of the North Saskatchewan River on the site of what is now Edmonton. Born Frank Bowsfield near Brampton, Ontario, in 1853, he took his mother's maiden name, Oliver, as his surname after a quarrel with his father. He left home at age twelve to become an errand boy in the print shop of the *Globe* newspaper in Toronto, apprenticed as a printer, and then headed west to seek his fortune.

Oliver settled first in Winnipeg, where he worked for the old *Nor'wester* newspaper, and then continued westward by ox-cart brigade for Fort Edmonton, where he hoped to start his own newspaper. He had inherited some money and used it to buy a small printing press in Philadelphia that he brought with him on the three-month journey from Winnipeg.

The printing press disappeared into the waters of the North Saskatchewan when a makeshift raft that Oliver built to cross the river broke apart and sank. He managed to salvage some of his other goods and used them to establish himself as a general merchant in competition with the Hudson's Bay Company, but his heart wasn't really in the retail business. When he noticed that telegraphed news briefs pinned to his store walls were attracting more attention than his merchandise, Oliver decided to take another shot at starting his own newspaper. He recruited the telegraph operator, Alex Taylor, to help him and they travelled to Winnipeg to buy a hand press. When they returned, six months later, the twenty-seven-year-old Oliver was married to sixteen-year-old Harriet Dunlop of Prairie Grove, Manitoba.

The first edition of the *Edmonton Bulletin*, a tiny newspaper with pages measuring five and one-half inches by seven and one-quarter inches, appeared on 6 December 1880. It pledged to offer the "most notable occurrences in the world at large and matters concerning the North-West Territories in particular." In the beginning, these amounted to little more than a listing of local produce prices, news of the comings and goings of local residents, and a large advertisement for Oliver's own store. However, it soon became a powerful advocate for what Oliver called the "rights of the pioneers." The settlers in the Upper Saskatchewan valley needed a champion and Oliver became their voice. With fierce rhetoric he railed against John A. Macdonald's Conservative government for alleged incompetence and corruption, and he condemned railways and land companies for speculating rather than investing in the development of the area.

Oliver's political career began in 1883 when he was elected to the council of the North-West Territories as the member for the Edmonton district. He fought for self-determination for the federally controlled territories, and wrote the act setting up the first public school system in the territories. He also introduced the secret ballot to the territories and became part of the group demanding that the territorial council become a representative legislative assembly with an elected speaker instead of an appointed lieutenant-governor.

At first a declared independent, Oliver gradually identified himself publicly with the federal Liberals (his daughter Claire Keefer said later that his "admiration for Sir Wilfrid Laurier amounted to idolatry"), and in 1896 he stepped into the federal arena as the Liberal MP for Edmonton. At that point, he was widely known throughout the territories for his belief that the future of Canada was in the development of the West. He was also known for his publicly expressed view that Natives should live in "a more congenial setting" than Edmonton and that they "would be a drawback to the country for an indefinite period." He was not alone in these sentiments. He was, in fact, espousing a very common and widely held set of beliefs in the frontier settlements of the West at that time.

As much a booster of Edmonton as he was a promoter of Anglo-Saxon superiority, he scorned the Slavic races as much as he did the Natives and other non-whites. Oliver used his newspaper and his position as one of two Alberta Liberals in the House of Commons to make sure that the northern city was chosen the capital of the province created in 1905. When Calgary sent a delegation to Ottawa to lobby for the new capital, Oliver responded by writing a letter to Laurier: "I submit that your government is still in honour bound to give the preference to where your friends are in the large majority, as compared to the place where your opponents are in the majority."

Edmonton was made provisional capital pending a vote of the new Alberta legislature. With its larger population, Calgary seemed poised at that point to vote the capital south. However, when it came time to draw up the province's twenty-five electoral boundaries, the job fell to Oliver and fellow Liberal MP, Peter Talbot. They ensured that the majority of constituencies were in Edmonton's orbit. The result was a sixteen-to-eight vote for Edmonton.

By then Oliver had been made the federal minister of the Interior and the minister responsible for Native affairs. He lobbied for the newly discovered hot springs and surrounding area at Banff to be granted to the people of Canada, thereby creating the country's first national park, and he supported the Canadian Northern and Grand Trunk Pacific railway projects to break the monopoly of the CPR. More controversially, by today's standards, he opposed "indiscriminate," i.e., non-British, immigration, and called on Natives to "surrender" their treaty-held lands and move to areas "near northern lakes" so that their lands could be free for development.

Oliver retained his Edmonton seat in 1911 when the Liberals were defeated but lost it in the 1917 election to war hero, Bill Griesbach, when Oliver took a renegade position against conscription. His stance was at least partly due to the loss of his eldest son, Alan, in the Somme fighting. Oliver ran again in 1921, when the Liberals regained power under Mackenzie King, but in the face of a rising tide of new farmers' groups in the West, Oliver lost to the Progressive Party candidate. Unable to cope with rising newsprint and labour costs, he also lost his beloved *Bulletin* newspaper, which continued to publish under new ownership until 1951. The last owner was businessman Max Bell who shut down the paper rather than give in to the wage demands of the printers.

With the Liberals back in power, Oliver's loyalty to the party was rewarded with a patronage appointment to the Board of Railway Commissioners of Canada, where he argued for better transportation to the West and remained chairman until he was seventy-five.

Oliver died in Ottawa in 1933 at age seventy-nine. Three years after his death, Alberta's Royal Commission on the Conditions of Half-Breeds concluded that the landless Natives of the Prairies were "constitutionally unable" to compete with white Albertans. By then Oliver was being remembered, in the words of the *Edmonton Journal*, as "one of the great men of the West." Today, the commemorative landmarks in his name in Edmonton include an Oliver neighbourhood, an Oliver school, the federal Oliver Building, and a bronze Oliver plaque in front of the Macdonald Hotel.

The Big Four

Financial backers of the first Calgary Stampede

Pat Burns 1855–1937

George Lane 1856–1925

Archie McLean 1860–1933

A. E. Cross 1861–1932

In the summer of 1912, four wealthy Alberta cattlemen—Pat Burns, George Lane, Archie McLean, and A. E. Cross—met at Calgary's exclusive Ranchmen's Club with an American cowboy showman named Guy Weadick. They agreed to put up twenty-five thousand dollars apiece to finance a wild west show that would, said Weadick, "make Buffalo Bill's Wild West Extravaganza look like a sideshow."

Weadick called his proposed event a "stampede" to set it apart from the other rodeos then popular throughout the American and Canadian West. With the backing of the four cattlemen, it was staged the following September but it didn't turn out to be quite the stunning success that Weadick had forecast. The weather was generally poor, and on the few good days that the rain stopped, the show had to be called off because of what historian James H. Gray calls "Weadick's managerial ineptitude." However, it did have enough commercial potential to convince the four cattlemen—known to this day as the Big Four—that they should try it again. In the process, they established an institution that—with characteristic Calgary hyperbole—is today billed as "The Greatest Outdoor Show on Earth."

Pat Burns

Of the Big Four, the biggest, in terms of commercial success, was undoubtedly Pat Burns, a farm boy from Ontario who struck it rich as an entrepreneur in Calgary, building one of the world's largest meat-packing and food provisioning businesses. Born near Oshawa, one of eleven children of an Irish homesteader named Michael

O'Byrne, Pat was raised on a farm near Kirkfield, northwest of Peterborough, and came west at age twenty-two to become a homesteader. To finance the trip, he spent a winter cutting trees in the woods of northern Ontario and accepted two rundown oxen in lieu of wages when his employer couldn't pay him the one hundred dollars he had earned. On the hoof the animals were worth seventy dollars, but by slaughtering them and selling the meat, Burns made $140. That became his first lesson in the economics of the meat business.

Burns initially settled in Winnipeg, spending six months working on the construction of the Canadian Pacific Railway to earn the money he needed to get started as a homesteader. He bought two oxen, a wagon, a plough, an axe, a scythe, and other equipment, and he homesteaded near Minnedosa in what is now western Manitoba. To supplement his small income from farming, he hauled surplus hay to Brandon to sell in the market square, bought and sold breeding stock, and used his oxen to break sod for other farmers. "Anything to make a dollar," commented his biographer Grant MacEwan.

During the 1880s Burns concentrated more on livestock dealing than on farming, and he pioneered the shipping of hogs by rail from Winnipeg to market in Montreal. He eventually sold his Manitoba homestead and began buying and supplying beef to the crews building a rail connection between Montreal and Saint John, New Brunswick, through the state of Maine. This was followed by a larger contract, furnishing beef to crews building a rail line between Regina and Prince Albert. The crews are said to have never complained about the freshness or quality of Burns's meat. He delivered the cattle on the hoof and slaughtered them on the spot.

In 1890, work began on a railway connection between Edmonton and Calgary. Spurred by the success of his earlier railway contracts, Burns moved to Calgary and became the beef contractor for the railway builders. On the east side of the Elbow River, he built a small slaughterhouse that doubled as his sleeping quarters, hired a full-time butcher, and had a shack that he called his office on Ninth Avenue East. When the Calgary-Edmonton line was completed, he began supplying beef to the crews building the southern extension from Calgary to Fort Macleod. He also shipped beef into the

Crowsnest Pass region, south into Washington state, east to the Kootenays, and deeper into the British Columbia interior.

In 1891, Burns availed of an opportunity to supply beef to Native residents of the large Blood Reserve south of Fort Macleod. The man who tipped him off to the opportunity was rancher George Lane, and the two went into partnership when Burns landed the Dominion government contract. This was the first working arrangement between two members of what would eventually be known as the Big Four.

George Lane

Lane, the only American among the Big Four, was born on a farm near Des Moines, Iowa, in 1856. At age sixteen he moved west to Montana to work on a ranch. A visit to Alberta convinced him it was good cattle country. His opportunity to move here came in 1884 when the North West Cattle Company, owners of the Bar U Ranch west of High River, asked the Sun River Stock Association in Montana to provide them with a capable cattleman. Lane was nominated for the job, and he became foreman of the Bar U at thirty-five dollars a month.

Lane worked at the Bar U for seven years, and then resigned to start ranching for himself on the Little Bow River, southeast of High River. At that point, he began running cattle in partnership with Pat Burns and furnishing beef as a buffalo-meat substitute for the Natives on the Blood Reserve.

The Burns contract to supply meat to the Bloods lasted for two years, and during that time, Lane is credited with saving the life of his partner. The incident occurred when the two were attempting to corral a long-horned steer, brought to the Burns slaughterhouse for butchering. The steer turned on Burns, knocked him from his horse, and then chased after him as he ran toward the corral fence to safety. Lane, seeing the seriousness of the situation, drew his revolver and dropped the steer with one shot.

After the partnership dissolved, Lane bought the Flying E Ranch in the Porcupine Hills of southwestern Alberta, and Burns began expanding his operations into British Columbia. His small Calgary slaughterhouse burned to the ground in 1892 but Burns soon rebuilt

it into a larger abattoir complex. At the same time, he started opening butcher shops in the mining communities of the Kootenays. By
1896, he had fifteen shops in the West Kootenay country, all helping
to relieve a glut of cattle east of the Rockies. Alberta cattlemen faced
a serious slump following their denial of entry to markets in the
United Kingdom, and Burns helped them out by opening up new
markets for them in British Columbia.

During the Yukon gold rush of 1898, Burns took on the challenge of delivering beef to the miners in Dawson City. He shipped
the cattle north by boat from Vancouver, then drove them inland to
the Lewes River where they were slaughtered. The carcasses floated
from there down to Dawson. Burns delivered mutton to Dawson the
same way.

During the early 1900s, Burns added a thriving pork business to
his cattle and sheep operations and established himself as the "meat
king of Western Canada" when he bought out the extensive holdings
of his biggest competitor, William Roper Hull. As part of that deal,
he acquired an extensive chain of retail stores in Alberta and British
Columbia and a four-thousand-acre ranch property in what is now
Fish Creek Park at Calgary's south end.

The Fish Creek property was one of several ranches from around
the Calgary area that Burns purchased during the first decade of the
twentieth century. While his other business interests eventually
expanded into such fields as lumber, mining, oil, fishing, and real
estate, it was as a rancher that he wanted to be known. That's how he
described himself in 1912 when he combined with Lane, A. E. Cross,
and Archie McLean to finance the first Calgary Stampede.

Lane, by that time, was the co-owner of the Bar U Ranch, on
which he had worked for seven years after he first moved to Canada
in 1884. He bought the property in 1905 for an estimated $220,000
and within a few years was boasting that it possessed the world's
largest herd of purebred registered percheron horses, the crème de la
crème of French breeding stock.

A. E. Cross

Cross was also well known as a rancher in the Calgary area, though he was probably better known as a brewer. Born Alfred Ernest Cross in Montreal in 1861, he trained as a veterinary surgeon and came west in 1884 to work as a veterinarian at the giant British American Ranche owned by fellow Montrealer Senator Matthew Cochrane and located near what is now the town of Cochrane. Two years later Cross branched out on his own as the proprietor of the A7 Ranche, so named because he was one of seven children, south of Calgary near what is now Nanton. He became active in community affairs and helped organize an 1886 agricultural fair that was the predecessor of the Calgary Exhibition and Stampede.

A bout of appendicitis took Cross back to Montreal for hospital treatment and when he returned to Calgary in 1891 he brought with him a diploma saying he had trained as a brewer's apprentice. That same year, Cross set the wheels in motion for the Calgary Brewing and Malting Company, the first brewery in what was then the Northwest Territories. He was also a founding member of the Ranchmen's Club, an institution that is now Calgary's oldest and most exclusive private club, celebrating its 110th anniversary in the year 2001.

In 1898, Cross entered politics as Conservative MLA for Calgary East. The following year, he joined the frontier aristocracy when he married Helen Rothney Macleod, daughter of Colonel James F. Macleod, the Scottish-born Mountie who gave Calgary its name. Cross continued to be active in community affairs, as a director and president of the Calgary General Hospital, as president of the Alberta Exhibition Association, and as president, in 1908–9, of the Calgary Board of Trade, later known as the Calgary Chamber of Commerce.

Archie McLean

The other member of the Big Four, Archie McLean, was a sitting member of the Alberta legislature when he joined Cross, Burns, and Lane to finance the 1912 Calgary Stampede. Born in southwestern Ontario farming country in 1860, McLean came west to Manitoba in 1881. There he established what was to become a long-lasting friendship with Pat Burns. In 1886, McLean moved to what is now

Alberta, and after working as a ranch hand for a few years, he became manager of the large CY Ranch near Taber.

McLean's political career began in 1909 when he was elected as a Liberal for the Lethbridge constituency. He was serving as municipal affairs minister at the time of the first Stampede and was public works minister in 1919 when the Big Four reassembled to finance the second Stampede, an event billed as the First World War Victory Stampede. Four years later, members of the Calgary Exhibition board decided to make the rodeo a regular feature of their annual agricultural fair and the need for private backing was no more.

Linked by a Legacy

The lives of the Big Four continued to intersect at different points during the following years. All maintained a link with the Stampede, as directors and volunteers, and three of the four—Lane, McLean, and Burns—were involved with the Bar U Ranch.

Lane owned and operated the Bar U until his death in 1925. McLean, who lost his provincial seat in 1921 when the United Farmers of Alberta swept the Liberals from power, became manager of the Bar U and he negotiated the sale of the property to Burns in 1927. Burns didn't really need another ranch—he already had thousands of his own cattle, scores of cowboys, and an estimated five hundred miles of fence lines to maintain—but he believed his old partner Lane would have wanted him to own it.

Burns kept the Bar U until his death in 1937 at age eighty-one. Calves were born on the Bar U, fattened at another Burns ranch, finished at a Burns feedlot in Calgary, slaughtered at a Burns abattoir, and sold in thirty-seven Burns butcher shops in southern Alberta and British Columbia.

Six years before his death, on his seventy-fifth birthday, Burns was named to the Senate by Prime Minister R. B. Bennett. Burns left an estate with an estimated net value of $3.8 million, close to one million dollars of which went to the province of Alberta as succession duty.

Cross and McLean predeceased Burns. Cross died in 1932 in Montreal, the city in which he was born, and he was buried in Calgary, the city he helped build. One of his last accomplishments in

Calgary was opening a kitchen on the Stampede grounds where unemployed men could receive hot porridge. His son, Jim, took over the operations of the brewery, which was later sold to Carling O'Keefe, then to Molson, and shut down in 1994. Alfred's daughter, Mary Cross Dover, became active in Calgary community life as a city councillor and wildlife conservationist.

McLean returned to ranching, in the Fort Macleod area, after he left provincial politics in 1921. He died in 1933 at age seventy-three. The *Macleod Gazette* described his memorial service as being "probably the largest funeral ever held in southern Alberta."

The Big Four were honoured collectively in 1959 when a large exhibits building bearing their name was opened on the Stampede grounds in Calgary, and again in 1963 when their portraits were hung in the Canadian Agricultural Hall of Fame in Toronto.

Individually, they are remembered as well. McLean, as public works minister, is credited with being the architect of Alberta's provincial highway system. Lane's name came to the fore again in the 1990s when the Bar U Ranch was designated as a national historic site and a fifteen-foot bronze statue of him was installed on the property. The name of A. E. Cross was given to a junior high school in Calgary, and his former residence in the city's Inglewood district is now a popular restaurant. The name of Burns is everywhere—on Calgary roads, on a cemetery, a rock garden, a downtown commercial building, and a baseball stadium. The biggest of the Big Four, as his biographer Grant MacEwan declared, has become a legend in the history of Western Canada.

Sir Frederick Haultain

Frontier statesman

1857–1942

When Alberta became a province in 1905 it was largely due to the lobbying efforts of Frederick Haultain, a Fort Macleod lawyer and territorial political leader whose contribution as a nation builder was subsequently forgotten. He remained a little-known figure in Canadian politics until 1986, when historian Grant MacEwan published a political biography to rescue Haultain from what he saw as undeserved obscurity. In his introduction to the book, *Frederick Haultain: Frontier Statesman of the Canadian Northwest*, MacEwan said he was stunned "that the name of a man who should be one of our political heroes had almost disappeared."

One reason for Haultain's virtual absence from the history books may be that he pushed for one big province extending from British Columbia to Manitoba rather than accede to a federal government proposal to have the region divided into what is now Alberta and Saskatchewan. Another reason may be that Haultain was denied any of the political leadership appointments that resulted from the North-West Territories becoming two provinces. After 1905, this man who had spent fifteen years in the territorial government and was described by *Saturday Night* magazine as the most able politician in the West, with "no rival in any other province nor in federal affairs," was no longer a force in Canadian politics.

His political career began in 1887, three years after he arrived in Fort Macleod and started practising as a lawyer. Born in England, Haultain moved to Canada with his family at age three and was called to the Ontario bar in 1884. He moved to Fort Macleod with the intention of forming a law partnership with a university classmate, but it never materialized, and Haultain instead found himself working as crown prosecutor for the area.

Haultain was elected in 1887 to the Regina-based council of the

North-West Territories as the member for the Macleod district. He soon emerged as the leader of the faction demanding that the federally controlled council become a representative legislative assembly presided over by an elected speaker instead of an appointed lieutenant-governor. Prime Minister John A. Macdonald quickly got the message and removed the lieutenant-governor and other non-elected persons from the assembly. Haultain became the assembly's first chairman—in effect the territorial premier—in 1891, and he remained in that position until the region attained provincial status in 1905.

The push for provincial autonomy began during the 1890s. The locally elected assembly had neither the power nor the resources to cope with the needs of a rapidly expanding settlement population. It didn't even have the power to borrow money. Only with provincial status could the territory acquire needed funds to cover the mounting costs of such essential services as roads and schools.

Haultain formally launched a five-year campaign for provincial autonomy in May 1900 with a four-hour speech in the assembly deploring the unsatisfactory constitutional situation of the territories. Along with a copy of his speech, the assembly sent a draft autonomy bill to Ottawa and requested that it be signed into law. When the Laurier Liberals refused to act on the request, Haultain, who had maintained a non-partisan role as territorial chairman, joined the federal Conservatives and began campaigning for the overthrow of the government. It responded by offering him an appointment as a judge, hoping this would remove him from the territorial political arena in which he was the dominant player. Haultain refused the offer. He had no intention, he said, of "deserting the ship."

In 1905, after his government was re-elected, Sir Wilfrid Laurier finally agreed to grant provincial status to the North-West Territories. Much to Haultain's disgust, he refused to make it one big province, because it would then occupy about 12 percent of the total land mass of Canada, and that was simply too large. Haultain protested that duplication of services and institutions would be unnecessarily expensive, but to no avail. Nor would Laurier agree to Haultain's demand that crown lands and resources belong to the new province or provinces. Haultain returned from his meeting with

Laurier saying, "The government has been acting like a big pig trying to keep the little pigs from the trough."

When Alberta and Saskatchewan became provinces, it was widely expected in the West that Haultain would be offered the premiership or at least the lieutenant governorship of one of them. However, the newly appointed lieutenants-governor were both Liberals and friends of Laurier, and the provisional premiers they appointed were also Liberals. As biographer MacEwan wrote, "The man with the best claim to statesmanship was conspicuously absent." Haultain's support for the federal Conservatives worked against him when the new provincial order was established.

Haultain, who had been living in Regina since first elected to the territorial council in 1887, chose Saskatchewan for his political activity from then on. He contested the province's first election in 1905 as leader of a new provincial rights' party but lost to the provisional premier, Walter Scott. Haultain also lost the 1908 and 1912 elections in Saskatchewan. As a non-partisan territorial politician, he had dominated elected public life in the region with his vision for a proud and democratic West but on the provincial level, his quest for power was thwarted by new immigrant settlers who tended to vote for the party that brought them to Canada.

Haultain left politics after his party's third defeat in 1912 and returned to the law as chief justice for Saskatchewan. In 1916, he was knighted by the King, and the following year he was elected chancellor of the University of Saskatchewan. He served as chief justice and university chancellor until 1939 when, at age eighty-one, he retired to Montreal and married for the second time. His first marriage, to the English-born daughter of a territorial lieutenant-governor, had been a marriage in name only because she reneged on a promise to live in Regina with him after she had spent time in England recovering from illness. However, Haultain remained faithful to her and sent much of his income to support her until she died in 1938.

Haultain died in 1942 at age eighty-four. A legal colleague in Manitoba wrote, "If the Prairies ever come to the time for monuments to their statesmen, the first choice should be easy to name." Instead, Haultain became the forgotten political hero of Western Canada.

Henry Frank Lawrence

Pioneer settler

1859–1941

The story of Henry Frank Lawrence exemplifies the saga of white settlement in the Canadian West during the 1880s. An English adventurer from Devonshire, he immigrated to Montreal in 1877 at age eighteen and four years later moved to what is now Alberta where he hoped to establish a homestead that "under ordinary luck and management will lead to modest independence."

Like many immigrants of the period, Lawrence had little money and none of the agricultural skills needed to be a successful farmer in Western Canada. He was, however, prepared to learn and to work hard. "Youth and thrift in this land can win its opportunity," he said.

His journey westward took him by train via Chicago to Brandon, Manitoba, which was as far west as the Canadian Pacific Railway could transport him at that time. He continued on to Fort Calgary by saddle horse. "The pace we made averaged about two and a half miles an hour," he said, over miles of dry prairie that were, "as cheerless as a brick field." His abiding memory of that trek was of the buffalo skulls "with the fur still showing" that dotted the prairie landscape. The Rockies, by contrast, seemed to him a "cheering and imposing sight."

Lawrence arrived at the tiny hamlet of Fort Calgary in the spring of 1882, a year before the railway arrived. He camped at the confluence of the Elbow and Bow Rivers, not far from a Hudson's Bay Company (HBC) trading post, and remembered thinking that the HBC employees already settled in the area "must have regarded with mixed feelings the now approaching influx of civilization."

He was known as a friendly soul who, according to a local newspaper correspondent of the period, "mingled with equal equanimity with the elite of the land and the cow hands who drifted up from the other side of the border." Lawrence's evocative account of his early years in the Canadian West, published in Toronto's *Saturday Night* magazine in 1923, suggests that he met almost everyone of note in the region at that time. His acquaintances included Fort Calgary commander Colonel James F. Macleod, Chief Crowfoot of the Blackfoot tribe, cattle king Pat Burns, pioneering farmer Sam Livingston, and frontier lawyer Paddy Nolan.

Lawrence spent ten years herding cattle on ranches around southern Alberta, saving up money to buy his own place. He was paid between forty and forty-five dollars a month and often spent up to eighteen hours a day in the saddle. "In bad weather, the nights are interminable," he said. But the warm chinook winds eased his discomfort, and the memory of many of his herding experiences remained with him forever.

He recalled one event in particular when he and another herder were assigned to recapture some cattle that had strayed into Peigan territory southwest of Fort Macleod. When Lawrence and his companion arrived at the scene, they discovered to their great relief that the stray animals had been picked up by another team of herders. "The whole prospect was most picturesque and appealing," he wrote. "The great silence, the marvellous clearness of the atmosphere, the river at our feet, the long spans of oxen and the covered wagons, which distance showed in miniature moving down to their encampment, and over all a glorious sunset sinking behind the mountains completes a picture of early life in the North West I shall never forget."

In 1892, with enough money saved to settle down, Lawrence returned to England to find himself a bride. Aboard ship he met Ellen Isabella Chapman of Wixley Hall, Yorkshire. In 1893 he ended what he called his "weary bachelor's life" by marrying her. In 1895, they settled along the Red Deer River northeast of Calgary. The following year, they moved a few miles west to begin ranching on an eighty-acre holding near Pine Lake. They called their spread Sabre Ranch. Their brand, resembling a small cavalry sword, was chosen by the Canadian Pacific Railway (CPR) for display in the Alberta Room of Toronto's Royal York Hotel as an "interesting example" of the brands of the early West.

Henry and Ellen raised six sons at Pine Lake and became active in local community affairs. Henry dabbled for a while in real estate in Red Deer, served as a police magistrate, and became a prolific writer of letters to and articles for newspapers and magazines. His 1923 article for *Saturday Night* magazine is characteristic. At that point, Lawrence had lived in Western Canada for more than forty years, and felt he had a thing or two to say about the way the region had developed. "Many mistakes for which we suffer today have been made in the past," he wrote. "The agricultural development of the country would have been sounder had it been confined to the main railway routes of the country, and further blocks of land taken in and branch lines built only as occasion warranted." Cattle ranching had fallen into decline because of bad decisions made by politicians, and the only way the situation could be remedied was by "putting into effect the knowledge that no political party has a monopoly on the brains of this province."

Henry Lawrence died in April 1941, at age eighty-one. His wife, Ellen, who served as organist for the Holy Trinity Anglican Church in Pine Lake, died in April 1947. She was remembered as a "delicate" soul whose "courage remained part of her great spirit until it soared in glad release from her tired body." Her six sons acted as pallbearers. The Sabre Ranch passed to the sons, and then to the grandsons. In 1996, a centennial commemoration was held at the ranch. In 2001, the third and fourth generations of the pioneering Lawrence family were living on the property.

Bill Herron

Oilman

1870–1939

When a major oil strike occurred in 1947 near Leduc, it was Calgary, not nearby Edmonton, which stood poised to become the future capital of Canada's oil industry. One reason for this was that Calgary had been rehearsing for the role for the previous thirty-three years—ever since an Ontario adventurer named Bill Herron ignited Alberta's first oil bonanza with a major find in Turner Valley.

Herron, who deserves to be known as the father of the petroleum industry in Alberta, had settled in Turner Valley in 1905 after running a logging business in northern Ontario. He made his living as a teamster hauling coal from the Black Diamond mine to customers in Okotoks. In 1911, he noticed gas seeping from rocks near a Sheep Creek crossing where he had stopped to eat lunch. A self-taught amateur geologist, Herron decided the seepage had to be something other than ordinary swamp gas.

Herron returned and camped on the site for several days later that spring to test his theory. Using an oak barrel and a piece of rubber hose to capture the gas, he filled two stone jugs and sent them to universities in California and Pennsylvania for analysis. The word came back that, indeed, it was not marsh gas but naphtha, a volatile petroleum derivative used as tractor fuel and popularly known as "skunk juice."

In September 1911, Herron paid eighteen thousand dollars to buy the surrounding land and mineral rights, owned by an illiterate Black Diamond farmer named Michael Stoos. With that purchase, the story of the Turner Valley oil field and the history of the petroleum industry in Alberta can be said to have truly begun. The farmer's "X" on the down-payment document was the symbolic mark that would signify future excitement, romance, and economic prosperity in Alberta.

It took more than a year of effort and several disappointments before Herron was finally able to persuade others to share his conviction that there was oil in Turner Valley. One of them was Archibald W. Dingman, an Ontario-born entrepreneur who had been involved since 1906 in the drilling of natural gas wells in southern Alberta.

Dingman accepted Herron's challenge of raising capital for the Turner Valley drilling venture. He found eight speculators willing to join him when Herron, according to local tradition, put on a fabled demonstration worthy of Phineas T. Barnum. The group travelled down from Calgary in 1912, reportedly to watch Herron fry bacon and eggs on a pan when he put a match to the Sheep Creek gas seepage.

The bacon-and-eggs story was later debunked by Herron himself, but no matter. It is typical of the mythology that has accumulated about the early years of the petroleum industry in Western Canada. Dingman and his colleagues did not need a gimmicky cooking demonstration to appreciate the potential of Herron's geological speculations and supporting mineral titles. The prospect of black gold in Turner Valley was enough to convince the potential investors, who included the future prime minister R. B. Bennett, his law partner James Lougheed, brewery tycoon A. E. Cross, and real estate promoters T. J. S. Skinner and A. J. Sayre. For twenty-two thousand dollars they acquired a 55 percent interest in thirty-two hundred acres of land and mineral rights that Herron had assembled in the immediate proximity of the gas seepage.

In May 1914 oil came gushing from the "Dingman Discovery Well," as the press dubbed it, marking the birth of a vibrant new industry in the grain fields and cattle country of southern Alberta. News of the discovery raced around the world, touching off a speculative frenzy. Stocks and money changed hands in Calgary by the barrelful. From makeshift brokerage offices, frantic promoters hawked shares in dozens of new oil companies.

Turner Valley soon became known as "Little New York," full of brawling roughnecks, poker games, dancehalls, and bawdy houses. At the Roxy Theatre a weekly "Ruffneck Dance" was held every payday, and one old-timer recalled, "You could always count on seeing a great fight. Most of the brawls were over some girl. I remember seeing an awful lot of blood spilled on that dance floor."

Herron soon found himself on the fringe of the oil-boom frenzy, however, because his syndicate partners had compelled him to surrender almost half his remaining interest in the land and mineral rights in return for their commitment to spend fifty thousand dollars on development. Then came the First World War, when outside investment capital dried up and drilling and exploration activity came to a halt. Herron moved to a farming property on the outskirts of Calgary where he said he would "work at an occupation that was less speculative until financial conditions improved."

Herron sold the farm in 1917 and returned to the cartage business. He worked sixteen teams of horses, hauling oil well equipment, barrels of gasoline, and other freight. He did this all through the 1920s and made enough money to buy himself a fine home in Calgary's upscale Mount Royal neighbourhood. During this same period, Turner Valley enjoyed its second oil boom and Herron reaped some of the benefits as the majority shareholder in a leasehold and drilling company named Okalta Oil Ltd.

In 1928, Okalta had a major oil strike near the banks of Sheep Creek, less than a mile upstream from the original gas seepages. It was Herron's finest moment. The property he had chosen sixteen years before, and had struggled to maintain, had at last vindicated his faith, optimism, and tenacity. Long known jokingly among his peers as "Never-Sell" Herron, he now commanded new respect because of Okalta's success.

During the 1930s, as sometimes happens in a boom and bust economy, Herron's fortunes took a turn for the worse, and his Mount Royal mansion was seized by the City of Calgary for non-payment of property taxes. He left for British Columbia's Cariboo country to try his luck panning for gold. He returned in 1936 when an entrepreneur named Robert "Streetcar" Brown uncovered in Turner Valley what proved to be the biggest oil find in Canada to that point. Herron held title to leases on land adjoining the Brown discovery. He sold some of his interests, paid off his city tax bill, recovered title to his Mount Royal home, and resumed his activities with Okalta Oil Ltd., which he ran with his namesake son. At the time of Herron's death in 1939 at age seventy, Okalta was one of Turner Valley's largest independent oil companies. It stood as a fitting legacy to a man whose dogged determination had contributed so much to the development of Alberta's first major oil field.

Ho Lem

Chinese community leader

1870–1960

The Chinese have been a part of Calgary life ever since the Canadian Pacific Railway (CPR) line construction crews first came through in the 1880s. They were not welcome in those days. Although quiet and law-abiding, they were unfairly denounced by white settlers as habitual gamblers and unsanitary transmitters of disease. However, they endured and thrived, mainly because immigrants such as Ho Lem were able to look beyond the racism and the discrimination toward a future of hope and opportunity in their adopted country.

There were fewer than one hundred Chinese living in Calgary, all of them men, when Ho Lem settled there in 1901. Most had worked as labourers on the CPR, and when the line was built, many stayed to run laundries and restaurants. They kept a low profile, especially after 1892 when a smallpox outbreak in Calgary was blamed on a newly arrived immigrant from Canton. After several smallpox deaths in the white population, riots erupted in downtown Calgary, with drunken crowds attacking Chinese merchants, beating them with cricket bats, and destroying property. Local police made no effort to intervene and the North-West Mounted Police had to be called in to quell the disturbances.

Ho Lem was thirty-one when he arrived in Calgary. A butcher's son from Canton, he was born in a clay shack, and later recalled with some amusement that his father's trade had little impact on the family diet: "We had rice for breakfast, rice for lunch, and rice and vegetables for dinner." Educated privately in the absence of public schools, Ho Lem attended school up to age eleven, learned to read and write, and studied the tenets of the Confucian belief system.

He managed a small farm after finishing school, married at age seventeen, and sold groceries door to door for ten years. The money wasn't very good so Ho Lem quit his job and decided to try his luck far across the sea in a country the Chinese called Gim-Sun, the

Golden Mountain. He settled in Vancouver first, worked in a fish cannery for six months, and then moved to Calgary where he heard he could get free English lessons at a Chinese United Church mission opening there.

Ho Lem couldn't find work during his first six months in Calgary, but the time was not wasted because it gave him a chance to learn the language and learn about western ways. He spoke English with a Chinese-Scottish accent and was one of the first Chinese in the city to cut off his traditional Manchu braid, adopt western clothing, and convert to Christianity.

The Golden Mountain was slow to yield up its treasures. The only job Ho Lem could find was washing dishes for ten dollars a month at a Calgary hotel located just south of the CPR tracks, where about half the city's Chinese population lived. He worked his way up to second cook, saved his money for five years, and then opened a restaurant, The Belmont, in partnership with the man who first hired him as a dishwasher.

By 1907, Ho Lem felt sufficiently solvent to send home to China for his wife, Hong Quo, and their son, Frank. The family lived behind the restaurant at the east end of downtown Calgary, just north of the CPR line that bisected the city from east to west. The beginnings of a small Chinatown had been developing south of the CPR line before this, but this situation changed when the Canadian Northern Railway announced plans to build a branch line through the section of downtown Calgary where one-third of the city's Chinese residents lived and worked. Faced with rising property prices and rents, the Chinese moved north of the tracks.

In 1910, eight of Calgary's Chinese merchants bought a downtown property where they planned to construct a two-storey brick building with eight stores on the ground level and apartments on the second floor. Local white residents complained, saying the Chinese should be moved out of the downtown and segregated from the rest of the Calgary community. Ho Lem lobbied on behalf of the Chinese restaurant owners at a meeting with the civic authorities, and the merchants were given permission to construct their commercial building. Over the next few years, the Chinese acquired additional property in the area and thus today's Chinatown came into existence.

As Chinatown grew, so did Ho Lem's fortunes. In 1917, he left the restaurant business behind, put a down payment on a commercial building in Chinatown, and established the Calgary Knitting Company. He ran that business until the Second World War, when the mill had to be closed due to a shortage of labour and materials. Ho Lem switched careers again and started selling insurance for Sun Life.

He did well as a salesman. His results earned him a vacation trip to Miami in 1952 and several industry citations. He consolidated his integration into the North American way of free-enterprise life with his memberships in the Canadian Manufacturers Association, the Canadian Club, and the Calgary Board of Trade. He also earned recognition as the first Chinese elder of a Canadian United Church congregation, Calgary's Knox United. In 1954, Ho Lem laid the cornerstone for the Chinese United Church in Chinatown, and also put up the $120,000 needed to build the church.

While Ho Lem thrived, his wife, Hong Quo, never took to Canada. She didn't like the life style and she didn't like western clothes. "In her mind, she was always going back," said Ho Lem. He, on the other hand, never intended to go back. "I have known from the very beginning that this was the country to live in." At the same time, he always maintained a keen interest in the political affairs of his native country. When the Chinese nationalist leader Sun Yat-sen visited Calgary in 1911, Ho Lem served as his host and helped Sun raise more than three thousand dollars for the overthrow of the Manchu dynasty. After Sun left, Ho Lem helped establish a local branch of the Chinese National League, an overseas extension of the Chinese republican movement that is still active in Calgary.

Ho Lem was ninety when he died in 1960. At that point, he was the acknowledged patriarch of Calgary's Chinese community and a devoted champion of ethnic assimilation and racial harmony. His name continues to be remembered annually when the Ho Lem Award is given for the best ethnic community float in the Calgary Stampede parade. "We all have to mix," said Ho Lem shortly before he died. He had come to Canada in search of his Golden Mountain, and despite discrimination and prejudice, he found it in the foothills of the Canadian Rockies.

William "Bible Bill" Aberhart

Teacher, radio evangelist, and premier

1878–1943

William Aberhart was one of the strangest political figures ever to appear on the public stage in Canada. In the midst of the Great Depression, he emerged from the obscurity of a high school classroom and a religious sect that he founded himself, preaching a new economic doctrine and promising a new utopia. He fulfilled none of his pre-election economic promises during his eight years as Alberta premier, yet the force of his personality was such that at the time of his death he still had more believers than doubters. The political dynasty he established—the world's first Social Credit government—remained in power in Alberta for another twenty-eight years.

Aberhart didn't become involved in politics until he was in his mid-fifties. Born on a small dairy farm in southwestern Ontario, he trained as a schoolteacher and for the longest time devoted his life to education and religion. He was principal of a public school in Brantford by the time he was twenty-seven, and simultaneously he was active as a lay preacher and Bible class teacher at various Presbyterian, Methodist, Baptist, and Congregational Churches around Brantford, Hamilton, and area.

In 1910, Aberhart moved to Calgary with his wife and two daughters after accepting an offer from Calgary public school officials to become principal of a new elementary school in the upscale Mount Royal neighbourhood. Five years later, he was appointed principal of the newly built Crescent Heights High School, a position he held for the next twenty years. He was known as a talented teacher and a very able administrator. Within a few years Crescent Heights was one of the largest and most successful high schools in the province, with students consistently scoring high in departmental examinations.

Aberhart started teaching a Bible class at Calgary's Grace Presbyterian Church shortly after he arrived. He moved to Wesley

Methodist after becoming embroiled in a dispute over his personal style. "Mr. Aberhart's doctrine is absolutely sound, but he simply doesn't know how to work or co-operate with others, and he doesn't know the meaning of the word 'love,'" said an associate.

The pattern remained the same after Aberhart moved to Westbourne Baptist Church. He continued to clash with some associates—particularly when he began introducing fundamentalist practices and doctrines into the church—but he had a growing and loyal congregation. By 1923 he was operating as a freelance evangelist, preaching to twenty-two hundred people every Sunday afternoon at Calgary's Palace Theatre. It was the old-time religion tinged with a measure of prophecy. Aberhart preached the literal word of the scriptures (as he interpreted them) and boldly warned of the divine judgment to come.

In 1925, Aberhart took his version of the Bible's teachings to the airwaves, broadcasting live from the Palace Theatre over CFCN Radio, a station heard throughout southern Alberta and in parts of British Columbia, Saskatchewan, and the northwest United States. Aberhart wasn't comfortable with the idea at first, fearing the radio broadcasts might cause the theatre audiences to dwindle, with a consequent reduction in the returns from the collection plate. Far from losing money, however, he established a wide financial base. Funds poured in by mail as response to his preachings grew.

In 1927, Aberhart took seventy thousand dollars from his coffers to build a Bible college in downtown Calgary. He named it the Prophetic Bible Institute, and used it for Bible classes, revival meetings, and missionary training programs. He also invested in CFCN, which turned five hours of its Sunday programming over to the charismatic preacher. In 1929, he finally parted company with Westbourne Baptist after most of the congregation had left the church, and he founded his own fundamentalist sect, the Bible Institute Baptist Church.

Up until 1932, the Aberhart message on the radio was evangelical not political. The *Back to the Bible Hour* broadcast provided spiritual inspiration and mental uplift for the many who were unable to attend organized church services, as well as for the thousands more who rushed home from the services to hear the deep and sonorous voice of this man who spoke of Christianity as a guide to daily living. They listened to Aberhart until 5 P. M. and then kept the radio on during the supper hour for the comedy of Jack Benny.

In the summer of 1932, Aberhart underwent a political conversion that has become legendary in Alberta history. Up to that point, he had been concerned primarily with enriching the spiritual lives of his radio listeners, but he couldn't ignore the fact that many of them were living in misery. Unemployed farm workers were reportedly eating gophers, and Aberhart was profoundly shocked by the suicide of one student who said he despaired of ever putting his education to good use.

During a trip to Edmonton to mark departmental exam papers, Aberhart found what he saw as the solution to Alberta's economic problems in the form of a book entitled *Economic Nationalism*. Written by a Scottish mechanical engineer and amateur economic theorist named Major Clifford Douglas, it argued that an inefficient capitalist economy, encumbered by debt and interest charges, left people without sufficient purchasing power to avail of the goods and services produced by the free-enterprise system. Douglas advocated that governments should step in, control credit, and distribute discount coupons and dividends—which he called "social credit"—to increase consumer purchasing power.

Aberhart knew that the free-market economy wasn't working. The evidence was all around him. On the one hand, there were thousands of unemployed, their incomes restricted to the amount of their relief cheques. On the other, there was a superabundance of goods that nobody was buying. The exchange mechanism had broken down. Aberhart became convinced that a chronic shortage of purchasing power was the cause and the Douglas proposals were the remedy.

Aberhart began to weave references to the Douglas theories into his religious broadcasts. The enthusiastic response from listeners told him he was on to something, but what was it, exactly? Whenever Douglas had been asked the question, he had talked about "the power of monetizing," and the "productive capacity of a given unit based upon that which is the real credit of the unit." For that reason, perhaps, he had been unable to find any political support for his theories in Britain. Aberhart was far more successful explaining the complicated political doctrine of social credit when he expressed it in biblical terms. Social credit, he told his radio listeners, was a way of throwing the moneychangers out of the temple.

Aberhart, like Douglas in Britain, had little success finding political support for social credit among the ruling establishment in Alberta. The United Farmers of Alberta (UFA) government refused to touch it after inviting Douglas to testify before the legislature. When Douglas expressed the opinion that the system could only be introduced as a federal initiative, the UFA leaders thought this would put an end to the discussion. However, it merely hardened Aberhart's resolve to make social credit become a reality in Alberta. Social credit was not yet a political party, merely a movement. Every meeting at the Prophetic Bible Institute began with a hymn and a prayer, but when the annual UFA convention of January 1935 formally rejected his motion to endorse a system of social credit for Alberta, Aberhart took the movement into the political arena. He announced plans to run a Social Credit candidate in every constituency in the provincial election later that year. If elected, a Social Credit government would print Alberta's own money to combat the power of the eastern banks, and pay a twenty-five-dollar monthly dividend to every citizen.

Few political commentators gave his new party a chance. On the eve of the August election, not one Alberta newspaper predicted a Social Credit victory. Aberhart felt differently, but he was not about to risk his principal's salary by running for election himself. It was only after the election, when a faithful Socred MLA withdrew, that premier-elect Aberhart became an MLA, representing Okotoks–High River.

The election victory, mirroring a trend typical in Alberta before and since, was spectacular. "Social Credit Landslide," said one headline, "New Party Registers Overwhelming Win in Provincial Election." Aberhart sent a telegram across the Atlantic to Douglas that likely would have sent a chill through the hearts of his supporters had they known about it: "Victorious. When can you come?" His message seemed to indicate that Aberhart had no idea how to put the Douglas theories of social credit to practical use. During the years following, he proved it.

The new Alberta currency—officially called Alberta Prosperity Certificates and popularly dubbed "funny money"—was issued in 1936 and quickly withdrawn from circulation when even Socred cabinet ministers refused to accept it as part of their salaries. The promised twenty-five-dollar monthly dividends were paid only once, to a handful of Albertans who had to sign away their life insurance in return. Almost every economic scheme Aberhart tried ended in failure, either overruled by the Supreme Court, disallowed outright by the federal government, or refused proclamation by the Alberta lieutenant-governor. Economically naive, Aberhart relied much too heavily on the untested theories of the eccentric and fascistic Major Douglas who, at the end of the day, could do no better than advocate a military coup for putting a social credit system into place in Alberta.

Did Aberhart know what he was doing? Seemingly not as far as economic reform was concerned, but he did it anyway. In his radio broadcasts he conjured up an image of a world freed from the bondage of money and financiers. With a hymn and a battle cry he articulated a new economic gospel for the Great Depression. His opponents were fornicators, grafters, and worshippers of the Golden Calf, not unlike those who betrayed Jesus Christ. To denounce them in such biblical terms was only right and just, said Aberhart, because "the day is past when religion should be put on the shelf during the week and taken down on Sundays."

Though his attempts at economic reform were virtually all failures, Aberhart was far from a failure as a political force. He did introduce good legislation affecting health care, labour, education, and oil and gas conservation; and for most Albertans, he remained a latter-day Moses who had been chosen by God to lead the children of the province out of bondage. After his death in 1943, they continued to re-elect his successors up to 1971, when Peter Lougheed's Conservatives came to power.

Aberhart died while in office, of cirrhosis at age sixty-four, and was succeeded by fellow evangelist and disciple Ernest Manning. Aberhart's death occurred in Vancouver, where he had gone for hospital treatment. There was no state funeral in Alberta. His family decided Aberhart should be buried in Burnaby because they felt his efforts in Alberta had not been appreciated. The Prophetic Bible Institute continued to operate under the presidency of Manning until 1951 when the building was closed. It was demolished in 1974 to make way for commercial development. An Eatons' department store now occupies the location.

Maude Riley

Child welfare advocate

1880–1962

The Alberta Council on Child and Family Welfare was founded in 1918 to look after the interests of children and mothers. Over the ensuing forty-six years, the organization became synonymous with the lobbying efforts of Maude Riley. She was a tireless community worker once described by a Calgary newspaper as "a plump little tyrant with winning ways who charms (or bullies) governments—local, provincial and federal—into passing legislation for the welfare of children."

Riley loved to tell the story of how she first became involved: "When my first baby was born in 1909, I was very ill, and I made a covenant with the Lord that if I came through I would devote my life to mothers and children. He kept His end of the covenant, and I've tried to keep mine."

Born Maude Keen in rural Ontario in 1880, she trained as a teacher and moved out to Calgary in 1904, the year before Alberta became a province. She lived with her older sister and taught at a one-room school with a reputation for being tough on its teachers. Before she arrived it had gone through four teachers in as many months. That didn't deter young Miss Keen, however. She faced her first class with a steely glare and a leather strap prominently displayed on her desk and quickly won over the children when they discovered she could skate, ride horseback, and throw an overhand curve ball.

She worked at the school for two years, then married Harold Riley, the deputy provincial secretary in Alberta's first provincial government. The couple moved to Edmonton. The students cried when she left. The parents were sorry to see her go too. Miss Keen had been the first teacher at the school who knew what to do with little boys who wrote profanities in their scribblers and bigger boys who chewed tobacco.

Maude Riley began her career as an activist social reformer as soon as she arrived in Edmonton. She joined the Local Council of Women, an organization whose members believed their maternal instincts gave them a particular advantage over men in working for social reform. She was part of a lobby group that met with Premier Alexander Rutherford to request new legislation that would protect the property rights of married women. Also in that group were Emily Murphy and Henrietta Muir Edwards, two of Alberta's foremost feminists who would later achieve national acclaim for their successful campaign to make Canadian women eligible for Senate appointments.

Riley continued her association with Edwards after she moved with her husband and daughter to Calgary in 1910. They served together on the National Council of Women, seeking improved legislation in the area of women's rights and child welfare, and fighting for votes for Alberta women. Through her volunteer work, Riley acquired a broad knowledge of legislation, politics, and the way governments worked, but she never considered entering politics herself. Women should only use the vote, she said, to have a say "in what laws should be made regarding the child and home life."

During the First World War, Riley headed up a volunteer committee that took on the huge task of collecting money, clothing, food, and other commodities for the relief of war-ravaged Belgium. She did this while continuing to be actively involved with the Local and National Council of Women and with a host of other organizations. As president of the Calgary Playgrounds Association, she lobbied for supervised playground areas for the city's children. As a vice-president on the YWCA executive, she took responsibility for developing recreational activities and making them available to women and girls throughout Calgary. She helped develop a hospital for the care of tuberculosis patients, and she campaigned for a home for the children of men killed and wounded in the war. Additionally, she served on the executives of the Women's Canadian Club, the Women's Christian Temperance Union, the Calgary Women's Literary Club, and the Calgary Symphony Orchestra.

Riley carried on her many volunteer activities and raised three children while her husband served overseas as a captain in the

Canadian army. When he returned in 1919, she was deeply involved in what was to become the greatest work of her life, seeking to make life better for the underprivileged children and mothers of her community.

The situation then was appalling. The infant mortality rate in Calgary was more than one in ten, and half of these deaths were attributable to the poor health of the mothers. Prenatal care was non-existent and medical care unavailable to those unable to afford doctors' fees. Milk was not clean, let alone pasteurized. An impure water supply coupled with minimal sanitation practices led to yearly epidemics of typhoid fever. Women had few rights and children even fewer.

Representatives from various Calgary organizations banded together in 1918 to form what eventually came to be known as the Alberta Council for Child and Family Welfare. They included people from the city health department, the volunteers who ran the city children's shelter, and members of different mothers' clubs throughout the city. The stated aim of the council was to improve the physical, mental, and moral development of the child. Riley became council secretary, thus beginning an involvement that would last until her death in 1962.

In 1923, Riley became president of the welfare council and she held that position, through thirty-seven terms of office, for the rest of her life. She refused to accept any payment for the job. When the members voted in her absence to give her twenty dollars a year to cover her expenses, she called for the motion to be struck from the records. She didn't need the money, she said, because her husband had a successful real estate and investment business, and she felt the money would be better spent on one of the council's programs.

By 1936, the welfare council was operating province-wide, with sixty member organizations representing an estimated eighty thousand women voters. Most of the politically and socially minded women in Alberta were involved, and several improvements in the lives of children and families were achieved. Some took years of constant lobbying and petitioning to attain fruition. It took almost twenty years, for example, before compulsory pasteurization of milk became a reality in Alberta, and several more years before health education became part of the school curriculum. "Eternal vigilance is the price of liberty," said Riley.

Promoting awareness of the council's work was an important focus for Riley. She produced a booklet on the care and well-being of children that was distributed through the school system and made its way into thousands of Alberta homes. The right of every child, she said, was to be "well born (i.e., to parents free from disease and alcoholism), well treated, well fed, well housed and well taught."

To the end, she remained true to her belief that women should play a supporting role within the existing male establishment, leaving men to deal with the politics and economics of the country, while women stayed home and cared for their children. "You don't have to be in parliament to get things done," she said. "All you need is sincerity, a reasonable purpose, and you can sell your bill of goods to any government—civic, provincial or federal." By looking after the children—the country's greatest natural resource—women placed the future economy of the country squarely in their own hands.

Riley was utterly single-minded in her pursuit of the improved health and welfare of the coming generation. She refused to accept arguments stating that governments suffering from the effects of two world wars and a major depression could ill afford such social reforms as she demanded. If money could be found for education, then it could be found for the physical and mental care of children. "The former is of little use without the latter," she said.

Her dictatorial ways don't seem to have bothered the other members of the welfare council with whom she served. She was their leader and they followed her. They accepted her autocratic, domineering manner because she got things done. Many of the social services, which are now taken for granted in Alberta, were first instituted through the perseverance and initiative of Maude Riley. She was often a step or two ahead of the legislators in terms of what she advocated, such as free hospitalization for maternity cases and better nutrition for school children.

She died in July 1962, just before she was due to receive an honorary doctorate from the University of Alberta. Always well off because of her investments, Riley left six thousand dollars to the Alberta Council on Child and Family Welfare. It disbanded in 1982 and was eventually replaced by the Alberta government's community-based Child and Family Services Authorities.

Riley's home in northwest Calgary was operated by the city as a children's shelter for several years after her death. It was officially named "The Maude Riley Home" and when demolished to make way for a larger structure, the name disappeared as well. There is a Calgary elementary school named after her husband, Harold W. Riley, a former MLA and Calgary alderman, but none named after her. Maude Riley appears to have been largely forgotten by the children for whose welfare she worked so hard.

Martin Holdom

Clergyman

1884–1972

Martin Holdom was typical of a certain kind of upper-middle-class British immigrant who came to Canada during the years leading up to the First World War. Raised to believe that Britain had the greatest empire in the world and that British institutions, customs, and people were superior to all others, Holdom saw himself as being part of a crusade to educate, uplift, and civilize "the colonies" to a lofty British standard. However, unlike some of his fellow immigrants, he soon came to realize that simply being a British gentleman was hardly enough to ensure success as a pioneer in Canada. In the process, Holdom came to accept what he never could while living in Britain. He realized that Americans and Europeans of non-British origin could make good settlers too.

Holdom came to Canada in 1909 at age twenty-five in response to a call from the Anglican Diocese of Calgary for young clergymen to serve the frontier. The son of a Buckinghamshire estate owner, he was educated in an elite boarding academy, at Oxford University, and at a theological college. After ordination he was appointed assistant curate at a large urban Church of England parish in Leicester.

When he left for Canada, Holdom had no illusions about what to expect. The Anglican Church of Canada's advertisements warned that life in the West would be hard and that prospective immigrants should be "strong, manly and gritty." Still, the payoff would be worthwhile. "There is the privilege of being allowed to take part in the building of what is destined to be one of the great nations of the world."

Holdom's destination, Castor, was Alberta's newest boom town. The Canadian Pacific Railway (CPR) had recently established a townsite there and the population had mushroomed in a few months from zero to 1,659. Because the railway extended no further eastward, Castor prevailed as the "head of steel," servicing a large farming area stretching almost one hundred miles to the Saskatchewan border.

The area was mostly populated by Americans, which didn't please Holdom at first. "It is sad to see this grand farming country being nearly all taken up by Americans," he wrote in a letter to his father. "Why do not more decent Englishmen come out here?" Later he would become more tolerant, but when he first arrived Holdom had all the pomposity that an English upper-middle-class upbringing could bestow on a young man. He instantly liked everyone he met who had the "right" kind of English accent, and he was critical of Canadian immigration policy that allowed the West to be populated with American, German, Russian, and Scandinavian land seekers.

Holdom changed his attitude when he discovered that the aggressive Americans and hard-working Europeans were better suited for life on the frontier than the indolent Englishmen of breeding who refused to adapt to local circumstances and spent their time complaining about life in "the colonies." The Americans and the Europeans were hard-working and self-reliant. So, for that matter, were the Canadian settlers and the lower-class English immigrants who knew what it was to work. Holdom gradually came to abhor the "nice boy" English types who played cricket and drank afternoon tea but "could not even clean their own boots." He began to understand why some employers in Western Canada posted signs saying that Englishmen should not apply. "People who cannot live without pianos and art had better clear out," said Holdom. "We have no use for them."

Holdom developed a genuine love of the Prairies. He became a cheerleader both for his adopted country and for his local community. Canada was the country of the future, he believed, and Castor could become a mighty city. He relished each new sign of civilization—his own church among them—and each example of community integration, including the Oddfellows' lodge and the curling club, which gave him a free membership in return for his service as club chaplain. Like his fellow settlers, he soon shared the local view that the Canadian Pacific Railway, while so essential for survival, was also a villain to both the homesteader and the town dweller. It conspired with the federal government to thwart local ambitions. "They did a great work in opening up the country, but they are a detriment now because they work simply to their own ends."

After a year, Holdom decided that he would never work in England again. Although the frustrations of ministering to a congregation scattered over hundreds of square miles were considerable, he never wanted to go back to the easy life he had left behind. He even turned down the opportunity to move to a more comfortable and wealthy parish in Edmonton, preferring to continue with his missionary work in an area defined by social isolation, lack of cultural facilities, material deprivation, and a harsh environment. The ability to endure without quitting, he concluded, was what would make this corner of the empire great.

He lived in Castor for five years. Toward the end of that time, in May 1914, he married Alberta-born Aldah Bryans, a Stettler schoolteacher. "She understands perfectly the hardships and the difficulties of frontier life," said Holdom. "An English girl is so uncertain; you never know whether she will take to the country or not." After four months of married life in Castor, Holdom suddenly resigned his position for reasons not specified in his letters. He accepted the rectorship of Mirror, a rural community located northwest of Stettler.

Holdom served at Mirror until 1919, and then briefly at Okotoks and High River. In 1920, he, Aldah, and their two daughters left the Diocese of Calgary for British Columbia where he served the parish of Surrey until 1925 and then Chilliwack until 1937. He served as canon of Vancouver's Christ Church Cathedral until 1943 and as honorary canon of New Westminster until 1949. After he retired from the church he wrote numerous pamphlets and articles about bird life in the lower Fraser Valley.

Holdom never returned to England. He died in North Vancouver in 1972, at age eighty-eight, after having created a good life for himself in Canada. His beloved Castor, where the population by 1996 had shrunk to 970, did not fare so well. It lost its status as "head of steel" when the railway extended eastward to the new divisional point of Coronation, and Castor no longer supplied the vast frontier to the east. Many Alberta towns shared Castor's fate. As historian Paul Voisey has written, "Built on exuberant expectations fired by settlement booms, they shimmered briefly in the prairie sun and faded in the ensuing twilight."

Monica Hopkins

Letter writer and rancher's wife

1884–1974

For many of the women of British origin who immigrated to Canada with husbands and family during the early years of the twentieth century, life on the frontier was difficult. Aside from the deprivation and economic hardship associated with homesteading, they had to adapt to what seemed to them essentially a man's country. When they wrote about it, in letters to family and friends back home, they spoke of the isolation and the loneliness. However, when Monica Hopkins wrote about her experiences as an English bride in southern Alberta before the First World War, she revealed an unremitting sense of exhilaration, cheerful optimism, and determination to find a place for herself as a woman on the frontier. "It is useless grousing over the inevitable," she wrote at the end of her first year on a Priddis ranch. "If you treat life as a joke and not take it too seriously, then you'll be happy here."

Monica came to the Alberta foothills in 1909, shortly after her marriage to Billie Hopkins, an Irish-born adventurer who had settled there seven years previously. Born Monica Maggs in Dorset, England, in 1884, she was the daughter of a Wesleyan minister father and a mother who did volunteer church work. The family lived in Montreal for three years when Monica was in her teens, and it was on the voyage from England to Canada that she met her future husband. They corresponded regularly over the next few years after Monica returned to England, and while Billie established his horse ranch on the banks of Fish Creek, nine miles southwest of Priddis.

Monica had some difficulty persuading her parents to consent to her marriage. They felt that life in the Canadian West would be too difficult for her. Her mother could see no hope there for a sheltered young woman who had never done sewing or laundry or prepared meals. Monica, however, had confidence in her ability to adjust. To appease her mother, she attended a domestic science class where she learned how to iron a man's starched collars and shirtfronts—hardly a useful accomplishment on the western frontier as she discovered later.

She found life without running water and other city conveniences to be hard at first. "I have been used to taps," she wrote in a letter to a friend in Australia. "A bucket with a dipper is new to me." She soon got used to cooking with a wood stove, doing the laundry in a wash tub, and preparing impromptu meals for local Natives who arrived at the doorstep unannounced whenever they were feeling hungry.

Letters became her lifeline to the outside world. There were days when she left Billie and his hired hands to fend for themselves because "I had more important things to do than cook. I had to write home and thrill the family with the story of my adventures." The mailman came to Priddis twice weekly to pick up and deliver, and she didn't want to miss him.

After a year on the ranch, Monica wrote that for a woman to survive on the frontier she had to "sink her own identity and take on her husband's interests." While this was true for her in that she functioned mainly as a helpmate while Billie built up his ranch business, it was also true that Monica went her own way whenever she wanted. She taught herself to ride a horse after observing that women "dependent on their men folk to take them about evidently do not get taken out very much." She played an active role in community affairs, serving as president of the local Red Cross chapter during the First World War and becoming the first woman to be elected to the board of the Priddis community hall in 1920.

By that time, Monica and Billie were living about two miles from Priddis, on a ranch where they raised sheep, poultry, and horses. They didn't have children but there was no lack of young people in their home because Billie suffered from arthritis and always needed someone to help him with the heavy work. Many young English boys started a new life in Canada working on the Hopkins ranch. English girls also got their start there, living at the Hopkins home and helping with household and general duties.

In 1943, when Billie was sixty-two, the couple left their ranch and moved to an acreage on the outskirts of Calgary, where they would be close to medical attention for Billie's worsening arthritis. During this period of enforced inactivity, Monica collected all the letters she had been writing to family and friends for the previous thirty-four years, and edited and rewrote them with a view to possible publication. However, getting material into print was not easy in those days, and the letters eventually ended up in the archives of the Glenbow Museum in Calgary.

Billie died in 1948 and Monica, at age sixty-four, decided to spend her remaining years in County Wicklow, Ireland, where her husband had lived as a child. However, by 1956, at age seventy-two, she was back in southern Alberta. She had no family left in England or Ireland, and here, in the country where she and Billie had spent their life together, she had many good friends.

Monica spent four years living in Black Diamond with a woman in her nineties who needed companionship and housekeeping assistance. She then lived in her own bungalow in Black Diamond and spent her last years at the Chinook Nursing Home in Calgary. She died in November 1974 in her ninety-first year and was buried in the Midnapore Cemetery next to Billie.

Seven years after her death, her letters finally appeared in print. The Glenbow Museum published them in 1981, in a book titled *Letters From a Lady Rancher*. "Although this is uniquely her story, it extends beyond the confines of one woman's experience," wrote editor Sheilagh S. Jameson in the introductory chapter. "It exemplifies the lives of other women who came to the foothills or similar frontier areas; women who suddenly found themselves in an unfamiliar setting, difficult and vastly different from that of their homelands."

William Irvine

Socialist politician

1885–1962

It seems hard to imagine it now, but Alberta during the 1920s was so receptive to left-wing reform ideas that one of Canada's most important socialist politicians of the twentieth century was able to launch a successful political career here.

His name was William Irvine. He was a clergyman from Scotland whose religious views were as radical as his political convictions. A fisherman's son from the Shetland Islands, he came to believe early on that Christianity and socialism were inseparable and interdependent. Like his hero, the British labour leader Keir Hardie, Irvine saw Christianity as being moulded by the different forms of society through which it passed and ultimately evolving into a socialist commonwealth. Irvine served as a Methodist lay preacher while in his early twenties and immersed himself in the writings of H. G. Wells and George Bernard Shaw, who influenced his thinking that socialism could be implemented through democratic—as opposed to revolutionary—means.

In 1907, a Methodist missions superintendent came from Canada to Scotland to recruit ministers for the missionary field in the Canadian West. Irvine signed on and immigrated to Winnipeg to begin his theological training. It took him seven years to complete it because he had little money and needed to work as a carpenter and farm labourer to finance his education.

He was ordained in 1914, after switching allegiance in the meantime from the Methodists to the Presbyterians. With his new wife, the former Adelia Maple Little of Shellbrook, Saskatchewan, he moved to the Rainy River district of southwestern Ontario to begin his pastoral work. With the agreement of his church board, he preached the Social Gospel, a reformist doctrine that endeavoured to apply Christianity to the collective ills of an industrializing society.

Irvine left the Ontario ministry in 1916 after being tried and acquitted by the Presbyterian church on a charge of heresy. He had shocked the conservative members of his congregation by preaching that the Bible was not infallible and that the principal purpose of religion was to minister to people in this life, not prepare them for some hypothetical afterlife. While his views were abhorrent to orthodox Protestants, they fitted in perfectly with those of the Unitarians, who invited him to become the minister of their church in Calgary. The church had only thirty-five members but the Unitarians believed Irvine would help the congregation grow.

Irvine found a comfortable niche for himself in Calgary. The church allowed him to pursue his social concerns as well as granting him the freedom to preach as he pleased. He became the centre of what some political observers termed "progressive" and others called "radical" thought and action within the Calgary community. In his first public address, reported in the *Albertan* newspaper, he said, "All political parties are corrupt. All newspapers, or nearly all, are cowardly. And the churches are either venal or woefully lacking in courage."

His ideas spread rapidly. Within five years, Irvine had become a leader in the Calgary labour movement, and more generally, a voice for social and political change. He was the driving force behind the Non-Partisan League, the radical farmers' organization that transformed the United Farmers of Alberta (UFA) from an economic interest group into a political movement. He was also the editor of a left-wing newspaper that began life as *The Nutcracker* and eventually became the *Western Independent*. Through his journalism and his 1920 book, *The Farmers in Politics*, Irvine became known as the chief intellectual spokesman for the emerging farmers' movement in Alberta.

In 1921, the year the United Farmers entered Alberta politics and terminated the sixteen-year reign of the Liberals, Irvine entered the federal arena as the Labour MP from Calgary East. The only other Labour candidate elected that year was J. S. Woodsworth, who later became the leader of Canada's first successful socialist party, the Cooperative Commonwealth Federation (CCF). "Mr. Woodsworth is the leader of the Labour group," Irvine told the House of Commons in his maiden speech. "And I am the group." They became part of a somewhat larger group a few years later when they joined the Ginger Group, a faction of dissident MPs who believed the party structure prevented them from properly serving their constituents.

Irvine became interested in monetary reform during the 1920s and was one of the first people to introduce Albertans to the Social Credit "new money" ideas of Major Clifford Douglas, the British economic theorist. However, Irvine never liked the way the Social Credit movement evolved under the leadership of William Aberhart—especially when Aberhart talked about printing Alberta's own money to combat the power of the eastern bankers. Irvine eventually became one of Aberhart's severest critics.

As a politician, Irvine was remembered by a fellow socialist, Amelia Turner, as bringing "joy and hope like an Alberta spring into our winter of discontent." An Ottawa newspaper characterized him as "a vision of virility and vehemence. He comes from that Prairie city where orators bloom like flowers in spring. A tall thin man, in the suburbs of forty (years of age), he stands erect, clean cut and clear spoken, with a voice in between the romantic actor and the preacher."

Irvine was defeated federally in 1925, but was elected the following year as the UFA member for Wetaskiwin. He waged an active campaign against the economic power of large corporations, and with his colleague, Woodsworth, helped lay the groundwork for the CCF. Irvine also helped establish the CCF's successor, the New Democratic Party.

Irvine served provincially for nine years, lost the 1935 federal election when Aberhart's Socreds came to power, and spent the next nine years on his farm in Wetaskiwin. He returned to politics in 1945, under the banner of the CCF, as the federal member for Cariboo, British Columbia. In 1949, he retired to Wetaskiwin. A decade later, he attempted two unsuccessful political comebacks while serving as party president of the CCF.

Irvine remained an ardent social activist to the end of his days. He died of lung cancer at age seventy-seven in 1962, shortly after completing work on a manuscript titled *Democracy—Fact or Fiction?* At that point he was a largely forgotten figure in Canadian politics.

His name did come to the forefront again in 1979 when Edmonton author Anthony Mardiros published a political biography, *William Irvine: The Life of a Prairie Radical.* However, as Calgary historian Howard Palmer noted some years later, Irvine was still not widely recognized for his contribution. "He was a very important figure in Alberta political history who died in relative obscurity and poverty."

Morris "Two-Gun" Cohen

Adventurer

1887–1970

Frontier settlements have always attracted drifters of unsavoury backgrounds. The Canadian West was typical in that regard. Colourful individuals stopped briefly in this region around the turn of the century. Among them were the outlawed Sundance Kid, friend to Butch Cassidy, who broke horses at the Bar U Ranch southwest of Calgary before resuming his more lucrative career as a train robber; and Ernest Dufault, a ranch hand from Quebec who served time in an Alberta prison for his part in a barroom shootout. Dufault later moved to Hollywood, changed his name to Will James, and became rich and famous as a cowboy writer and artist. Perhaps the most colourful of all was an English adventurer named Morris Cohen who became a bodyguard to the Chinese revolutionary leader Sun Yat-sen. Cohen earned the nickname "Two-Gun" because wherever he went he always packed two pistols that he wasn't afraid to use.

Born in Poland to a Jewish couple who fled to England to escape persecution, Cohen grew up in poverty in East London. He was arrested at age ten for picking pockets, sent to reform school for six years, then shipped to Western Canada to work for a homesteader at a Jewish farm colony in Wapella, Saskatchewan. He abandoned farming after a year and wandered throughout the West, picking pockets and hustling as he went. He spent much of his time in Chinese gambling dens, worked briefly as a carnival barker, and served time in a Winnipeg jail for carnal knowledge of a girl under sixteen for whom he was a pimp.

Cohen likely would have been forgotten by history, but in 1909 he stumbled into an armed robbery at a Chinese restaurant in Saskatoon, a fluke that saved his name from oblivion. He knocked the villain out and that earned him the respect of the Chinese community and a career in the Chinese revolution. The restaurant owner, who supported the republican movement in China, invited Cohen to attend a clandestine meeting in Calgary's Chinatown where he was granted membership in the secret Tong Society, an anti-Manchu empire organization devoted to the liberation of the Chinese people.

Cohen remained in Calgary, making an illegal living as a gambler, until the local vice squad made things too hot for him. He moved to Edmonton, sold real estate for the National Land Company, continued gambling on the side, contributed to the local branch of the Chinese Nationalist League, and became recognized as a spokesman for Edmonton's Chinese community. One Edmonton newspaper reported, "Mr. Cohen is in close touch with Chinese affairs here and knows the men of the orient probably better than any man in Edmonton or in western Canada." Another newspaper spun a fabulous tale relating to his background. "Mr. Cohen is a highly intelligent American with a long residence in China, who speaks fluent Cantonese and is a mason of high degree."

Having sway with the Chinese helped Cohen establish important political connections in Edmonton. He became friendly with Charles W. Cross, the province's first attorney general, who paved the way for Cohen to become a commissioner of oaths. Cohen used that office to help Chinese immigrants become naturalized.

The bottom dropped out of the Edmonton real estate market at the start of the First World War, and that left Cohen without any income except for the limited amount he could still make from gambling. However, the war opened up a new opportunity for him. He joined the 218th Overseas Battalion, was made an acting sergeant, and moved to Calgary to do his training. He had numerous skirmishes with the law while learning to be a sergeant at the Sarcee Camp, located on the southwestern outskirts of Calgary. The local newspapers referred to "his weekly appearance" whenever he went to court to answer a charge of disorderly conduct after a night of carousing at the King George Hotel.

In October 1916, Cohen was one of thirteen soldiers charged with disturbing the peace after a tussle with Calgary City Police. He conducted his own defence. "Sergt. Cohen shows surprising knowledge of court procedures," reported the *Calgary Herald*. The knowledge paid off. Cohen was acquitted.

Cohen served overseas during the last part of the war, saw action in Belgium, returned to Edmonton, and opened his own real estate office. He dabbled in oil and mining investments and tried to achieve a measure of respectability by serving on the executive of the Great War Veterans' Association. However, his old habits soon caught up with him. In 1920, he was tried and acquitted on a charge of using his office as a gambling den. In 1922, he was tried and again acquitted on a charge of illegal gambling. By that time, Cohen was ready to move on. He packed his bags and set sail for China, where he hoped to work for Sun Yat-sen, who was then attempting to unite the various political forces in China into a Leninist-style party after he had been toppled from power by a warlord named Yuang Shikai. Cohen arranged a meeting with Sun in Shanghai through a New York-born journalist who worked for Sun's English-language newspaper, *Shanghai Gazette*, and Cohen was given a job as one of Sun's bodyguards.

Cohen quickly became one of Sun's main protectors, saving his boss's life on several occasions. After being hit in the arm by a bullet during one attempt on Sun's life, Cohen began carrying two guns for protection, one on his hip and another in a shoulder holster. This attracted attention among Shanghai's western community who were already intrigued by this westerner who consorted with the Chinese. They started calling him "Two-Gun" Cohen. His nickname was born.

In 1925, Cohen came back to Canada to buy weapons for the revolutionary cause. He inflated his credentials to make himself a general in the nationalist army—despite the fact that he spoke not a word of Chinese—and impressed the Edmonton newspapers, which described him as "the right hand man of the president of the South China republic."

Sun died while Cohen was in Canada, at which point Cohen switched his loyalty to the new Chinese leader, Chiang Kai-shek. To the western press, Cohen made it seem as if he were an important force in southern Chinese politics. In reality he was little more than an errand boy, delivering messages for a series of revolutionary bosses in Canton and Shanghai and acting as a courier to accompany important officials passing through Canton and Hong Kong.

When Japan invaded China in 1937, Cohen joined the war

effort, smuggling arms and raising money for the China Relief Fund. When Hong Kong fell in 1941, Cohen was captured and sent to an internment camp. He was released two years later in a prisoner exchange and came back to Canada, settling in Montreal. In 1944, he married Ida Judith Clark, the owner of a Montreal dress shop. They spent their honeymoon in Lake Louise and Calgary, and spent much of the trip promoting the beleaguered Chinese government.

That was Cohen's last visit to Alberta. He spent the next few years making frequent trips back and forth from Montreal to China until the communists took over in 1949. Since he spent so little time at home, his marriage understandably failed. During the early 1950s, he and Judith divorced. Cohen moved permanently to England to live with a sister, and published a volume of memoirs that proved to be mostly fictitious. He made a few more trips to China during the years following, and helped Rolls Royce negotiate sales of its aircraft engines to the Chinese. In May 1960, he made one final visit to Canada, to appear as a mystery guest on the television show *Front Page Challenge*.

Cohen died in London in 1970 at age eighty-three. In 1997, New York author Daniel S. Levy published a well-researched, well-documented biography, *Two-Gun Cohen: A Biography*, which corrected all the errors in Cohen's own account and concluded that he was drawn to China in much the same way that he had been drawn to Alberta a dozen years before. "China between the wars was the Wild East," wrote Levy. "It was the last great frontier, filled with adventurers and fortune seekers, offering them the freedom to range and look for what they could take. Cohen seemed made for such a land."

Karl Clark

Oil sands scientist

1888–1966

The Athabasca oil sands of northern Alberta play a significant role in Canada's petroleum industry. They supply 12 percent of the country's entire crude oil requirements, and, as other conventional sources of oil and gas dry up, they provide Canada with an enviable protection against possible petroleum shortages in the future.

Close to fifty years of research and development took place before the oil sands became a commercially viable source of energy for Canada. Many people were involved in this work, but the person who made the biggest contribution was undoubtedly Karl Clark. Clark was an Ontario-born research chemist with the federal mines department who, during a field trip to Western Canada shortly after the First World War, saw the oil sands as a possible solution to road problems common in the Prairies in wet weather.

Clark noted that in dry weather the clay used for road building throughout the western provinces was almost as good as concrete. But, when it rained, the clay absorbed the water and swelled up, turning the unpaved roads into quagmires. Vehicles either slid off the road or became hopelessly bogged in the ruts. Clark reasoned that waterproofing the roads with oil was the answer. Oil was a natural water repellent and perhaps the Athabasca sands could be used as this source of oil. Finding a way to separate the oil from the sands thus became his life's work. "Once the tar sticks to your boots, you can never get it off," said Clark.

The son of a languages professor at McMaster University, then located in Toronto, young Karl was an indifferent student in high school and seriously considered dropping out and getting a job. However, his father would not hear of this and insisted that Karl remain in school. Because chemistry was the one subject he did enjoy, Karl decided to focus on this at university. He continued his studies, going so far as to earn a Ph.D. in chemistry at the University of Illinois.

After being rejected for military service in the First World War because of poor eyesight, Clark accepted a position with the Geological Survey of Canada, analyzing and classifying soils taken from different parts of Canada where roads were to be built. As an additional scientific assignment he was asked to provide a critical review of a 1917 research study done by the federal mines branch on the proposed commercial development of what were then known variously as the "bituminous sands" or the "tar sands" of northern Alberta. Clark declared the research to be inconclusive and muddled, and he began to see this as an area where he might make a contribution. By 1920, he had discovered a possible method of separating oil from the sand through the use of a chemical additive.

The University of Alberta provided Clark with the means to continue experimenting with ways to separate the oil from the Athabasca sands, after the federal mines department shut down the experimentation for unspecified reasons. Henry Marshall Tory, founder of the University of Alberta, was a champion of resource development and he saw the university as serving the province's industrial needs in a practical way as well as being a teaching institution. University scientists were already applying their expertise to the operation of farming and coal mining in Alberta. Investigating the potential of the oil sands was an enticing prospect because, among other things, it might eventually lead to the establishment of a chemical industry, as had happened with coal tar in Europe during the second half of the nineteenth century.

Tory offered Clark a position as research professor at the University of Alberta after he heard that Clark had achieved some success extracting oil from the sands. Clark accepted the position and in September 1920, accompanied by his wife and infant daughter, he came to work at what is now the Alberta Research Council. To facilitate Clark's work, Tory had six tons of oil sands transported from the Athabasca region and stockpiled on campus next to Clark's laboratory. By early 1921, Clark had developed a crude version of the hot-water method still used today for oil sands extraction. He used the family washing machine as part of his experimentation.

Clark's next step was to move the separation process from the lab to an experimental plant capable of batch operation. With his lab assistant, Sidney Blair, he designed and built a plant in the basement of the University of Alberta's mechanical building. It worked very well, and its success provided the impetus for Clark and Blair to design a larger plant to demonstrate the process as a semi-commercial, semi continuous operation. That plant, built on the northern outskirts of Edmonton in 1924, didn't work well at first. However, after extensive modifications by Clark, it improved, and by 1925 it was being hailed across North America as the first continuous separation plan for bituminous sands ever built and operated. The following year, Clark and Blair published a major report on their work, concluding that the ultimate use of tar sand oil would be as a feedstock for oil refineries.

In 1930, the work moved closer to the source of the raw material with the opening of the Clearwater separation plant on a tributary of the Athabasca River, near the town of Fort McMurray. It operated well but inconsistently, and it took Clark two years to achieve more uniformity in the separation results. By then the Great Depression had hit Alberta with a vengeance, and all money for oil sands research had dried up. As Clark noted afterward, the fundamental research questions had then been answered. The next step was to turn the fruits of the experiments into commercial development.

It took another thirty-seven years before large-scale commercial development became a reality. There were a few small-scale attempts but they struggled with scant success, largely due to underfunding. Clark stepped away from oil sands research and retrained as a metallurgist. Blair moved to Chicago to work for Universal Oil Products. However, with the re-establishment of the Research Council in 1942, Clark was able to return to oil sands research. He started investigating such questions as how to make the heavy tar sand oil fluid enough to pass along transmission lines and how to extract the oil from sands located too deep beneath the surface for conventional strip mining.

During the late 1940s, Clark served as technical consultant for the provincial government's Bitumount project, located sixty miles downstream from Fort McMurray; a pilot plant built to experiment with a cold-water separation process. Shortly after it opened, the government commissioned Clark's former associate Sidney Blair to make a comprehensive study of the costs involved in extracting and transporting oil from the sands to refineries in southern Ontario. Blair concluded, after a year of study, that progress with this immense oil deposit in northern Alberta was "entering the stage of possible commercial development." That report, released in 1950, is said to have spawned the commercial industry that exists today.

Clark retired in 1954, when he turned sixty-five, but he continued his association with the Alberta Research Council in a part-time capacity for another nine years. By that time, plans for constructing the first large-scale oil sands plant were well underway. Between 1950 and 1965 Clark was much in demand as a mentor for the increasing numbers of graduate science students drawn to the new field of oil sands technology. He also served as an advisor to the Great Canadian Oil Sands—now Suncor Energy—the company that was to bring his lifetime of research into large-scale commercial reality.

In 1965, Clark witnessed the turning of the first sod of the Great Canadian Oil Sands plant in Fort McMurray. He died of cancer in December 1966, just nine months before Premier Ernest Manning cut the ribbon to open the big plant. By that time Clark was widely recognized within the petroleum industry as the developer of the hot-water process now used in different forms by Syncrude Canada and Suncor Energy. But with the joy of success came sadness at seeing the landscape of his beloved Athabasca country scarred by strip mining. Clark confided to his daughter, shortly before his death, that he had no wish to ever return to the scene.

Elizabeth Sterling Haynes

Drama educator and community theatre pioneer

1897–1957

Community theatre in Alberta owes a big debt to Elizabeth Sterling Haynes. She left her imprint on the amateur drama scene across the province. During the 1920s, she helped organize a provincial drama league that became a model for the Dominion Drama Festival, the national amateur theatre competition that bridged the 1930s' collapse of foreign touring and the post-war emergence of Canada's professional theatre. During the 1930s, as the University of Alberta's first travelling drama specialist, she taught and influenced hundreds of theatre enthusiasts who went on to leave their own imprint on the province's drama scene. Elizabeth Haynes's vision of the theatre as a spiritual and populist form of human expression resonated most forcefully in a province defined in some manner by the conventions of its religious and populist institutions.

She came to Alberta in 1922 after cutting her theatrical teeth in Toronto. Born Elizabeth Sterling in Durham, England, in 1897, she moved to rural Ontario with her parents in 1905 and started attending the University of Toronto in 1916. At that point, homegrown theatrical activity in English Canada was confined mainly to university campuses because the bulk of the population was preoccupied with the concerns of the First World War.

Sterling began her theatrical career as an actress with an all-female drama club at the University of Toronto. Then she became one of the first to tread the boards at Hart House Theatre, a campus playhouse that accommodated both student and community drama groups and evolved over the years into a crucible for emerging young actors on their way to professional careers. At Hart House, Sterling was strongly influenced by Roy Mitchell, a director who inspired in her a sense of theatrical mission and purpose. For Mitchell, theatre was something more than costumes and props and makeup. It was a kind of "holy ground," a temple of the human spirit rooted in ritual and religion. The essence of a play lay not so much in the words or in the way they were presented but in the manifestation of the play's living soul in performance. The director's job was to help actors find that intangible soul, make the invisible incarnate, and turn it into something real on stage.

Sterling became an immediate convert to the Mitchell religion of theatre. Her theatre, like his, would be rooted not in the externals of the craft but in the spiritual forces that lie within. Inner awareness would come first; the lines, blocking, and movement would come later. As one of her actors said, "You would practically have to write an essay on this character, on where he came from, and all his ancestors and everything else" before being allowed to speak the words the playwright had written for the character.

Sterling taught school in upper New York State for a year before starting to put her theatrical theories into practice. In 1921, she returned to Ontario to marry Nelson Haynes, a dentist and fellow University of Toronto graduate. The following year, they moved to Edmonton, where Nelson established his practice and Elizabeth started directing productions at the University of Alberta. Because of her Hart House experience, she was warmly welcomed by the campus dramatic society. Over the next decade, she introduced university audiences to a variety of challenging plays—including Leonid Andreyev's *He Who Gets Slapped* and Elmer Rice's *The Adding Machine*—all well-produced and acted.

Haynes's reputation as a director was such that, beginning in 1929, she was invited to teach drama to schoolteachers at the joint summer school sessions of the university and the provincial department of education. At the same time, she was appointed artistic director of the newly formed Edmonton Little Theatre, a job that turned out to be a mixed blessing for her. On the one hand, she was able to light up the Edmonton stage with the works of such major playwrights of the period as Shaw and Coward. On the other, she had to look after the business and financial side of running a theatre, and that didn't appeal to her at all.

In 1930, Haynes helped stage a provincial drama festival in Calgary that was the first of its kind in Canada. The following year, she began a series of weekly talks, entitled *The Story of the Theatre*, on

CKUA Radio, which was then the University of Alberta's campus radio station. These talks brought her theatrical message to audiences throughout the province. She carried the message still further as a director and actress with the Chautauqua travelling tent shows, playing forty Alberta and Saskatchewan communities in a single summer. All of these activities made Haynes the obvious choice for the University of Alberta's first full-time travelling drama specialist when the Carnegie Corporation of New York gave the university a three-year grant to develop drama in the province.

Because of the Carnegie grant, Haynes was able to play a pivotal role in founding what is now the Banff Centre for the Arts. She was also able to foster the growth of community drama in rural Alberta, and simultaneously, to help revamp the Alberta high school curriculum to include drama. "From the schools we may expect a powerful impetus towards the growth of a vital national drama," she said.

The growth of drama in the rural areas, while influenced to some extent by Haynes's promotion of drama as a vehicle for self-expression and development, also had its own dynamic, linked to the social and economic conditions of the period. The Great Depression brought rural people together in an atmosphere of sharing and helping one another, and drama did the same. It helped build a sense of community, especially when presented under the auspices of the institutions most concerned with improving the quality of rural life—organizations such as the Women's Institute and the United Farmers of Alberta.

The Carnegie project was extended for two years, finishing at the end of 1937. At that point, Haynes was invited to New Brunswick to run the drama division of a newly established government summer school for teachers. The summer assignment was extended into the fall and Haynes found herself combining the work of rural community drama and educational drama just as she had in Alberta. By the end of her year in New Brunswick, Haynes had built a province-wide school festival movement and helped a number of communities develop productions for presentation at the Dominion Drama Festival.

During the 1940s and into the 1950s, deteriorating health plagued Haynes, but she remained actively involved in the Alberta drama scene as a director and teacher. She wrote and produced radio plays, ran community drama programs, and helped create scholarships for promising young actors.

In 1955, with her health steadily worsening, Haynes left Alberta with her husband to return to Ontario. There she continued to conduct drama classes and direct plays. She died in the spring of 1957 while casting for a production of Thornton Wilder's *Our Town.* "This play formed a fitting epitaph to a career dedicated to the human spirit and the small town," wrote Moira Day and Marilyn Potts in a 1987 essay for the magazine *Theatre History in Canada.*

Two years before her death, Haynes had written an article for the *Alberta Golden Jubilee Anthology,* in which she told about her dream for theatre in Alberta. "Some day, perhaps, we will truly build our own theatre. Alberta playwrights will create drama—strong and colourful and moving as the province itself—and Alberta actors will translate it into life, all over Alberta, for thrilled Alberta audiences." When she died, her dream was still unrealized. Today, it's much closer to being reality. Edmonton's Sterling Awards are named in her honour.

Gladys McKelvie Egbert

Piano teacher

1897–1968

Gladys Egbert was a true cultural patriot, loyal to Canada, loyal to Alberta, and loyal to Calgary. She had the talent to be very successful on the international stage as a concert pianist, yet she chose instead to become a music teacher, and a very good teacher she was. During the 1960s, her name was known in musical circles across Canada as the teacher in Calgary who taught the winners of the CBC's annual Competition for Young Performers.

Her involvement in music began shortly after her land agent father and schoolteacher mother brought her from Brandon, Manitoba, to Calgary as a child at the turn of the century. At age six, Gladys McKelvie rode her pony along unpaved roads and tied it to a rail outside the home of Annie Costigan, Calgary's first music teacher. The pony waited patiently while Gladys played her scales and Conservatory pieces.

She demonstrated a remarkable talent for performance from her earliest years. At age twelve, she won a three-year scholarship to the Royal Academy of Music in London after receiving a gold medal from the Academy for the highest marks ever given to a student taking the Academy examinations in Canada. Gladys was the first Canadian ever to win a scholarship to the Academy and the youngest student ever to do so.

Gladys's mother had to return to Calgary to look after her ailing husband, so Gladys lived in London by herself after the first year of her scholarship. Despite this, Gladys showed extraordinary dedication and perseverance. She studied with many renowned musicians whose names could be found on the jackets of records and on the covers of books of sheet music. Gladys later went on to study at the Juilliard School of Music in New York with a one-time pupil of Jan Paderewski, the famed Polish pianist and statesman.

Her father died in 1919 and Gladys decided her mother's welfare was more important than her desire to make a splash in international music circles. She turned down both the chance of a concert career and the opportunity to teach at Juilliard, returning to Calgary to begin providing the highest quality musical education to the few who might benefit from it. Years later, Gladys said it took as much work and dedication to become a good teacher as it did to become a good performer. A person could do one or the other, she said, but not both.

If Gladys had any regrets about giving up the bright lights of London and New York for the limitations of a city with a small talent pool, she never expressed them. The music teachers in Calgary who made it possible for her to experience the culture of the larger world had fostered her talent. Now she had a chance to create the same possibility for others.

Four years after returning to Calgary, Gladys married Bill Egbert, a young Calgary lawyer who later became a judge of the trial division of the Supreme Court of Alberta. They lived next to the Elbow River in an imposing red-brick house with two pianos in the living room to facilitate the playing of duets. Former student Marilyn Engle, who later went on to be a concert pianist and teacher herself, has described the living room as a world filled with excitement, adventure, and glamour. Gladys—known affectionately to her students as "Mrs. E."—made up lyrics for the pieces her students were playing, sang along, and danced to the minuets and waltzes. She brought her students back in time to the period when the composers lived, describing how they looked and what they wore. "I will always be indebted to Mrs. E for opening the doors and leading me through into that world," wrote Engle in an essay published in the book *Woman as Artist: Papers in Honour of Marsha Hanen.*

Although teaching, being a mother to two children, and attending to her mother's needs kept her close to home, Gladys maintained her international contacts with regular trips to New York to take piano classes with the dean of the Juilliard School, Ernest Hutchinson. He had once taught her how to combat performance jitters by keeping in mind that she had played the piano pieces flawlessly in rehearsal, and Gladys passed on the same tip to her students.

In 1936, Gladys was elected a fellow of the Royal Academy of

Music, the first North American to be so honoured. It was the London Conservatory's way of saying that its star pupil's contribution to international music had not stopped when she became a teacher in Calgary. Her success could be measured by the high marks scored by her students in the Royal Academy examinations given in Canada.

Her success seems to have been linked in some manner to her method of adding impromptu verses to the melodies of the piano pieces and having her students sing them silently while playing. The purists might knock this method as a violation of the time-honoured dictum that instrumental classical music should stand on its own, but for Gladys's students, it was a powerful heuristic tool. By focusing on the verse, the students were able to play with great enthusiasm and conviction. "By these means and others like them, Mrs. Egbert imparted a fundamental understanding of style," wrote Engle. "We were given the opportunity to acquire this understanding in a unique context, one where delight grounded the learning of principles. Can any teacher give students a greater gift?"

During the 1960s, Gladys achieved some of her greatest successes as a teacher, with her students winning regularly in local, provincial, and national competitions. Some travelled great distances for their weekly lessons, and several achieved the concert stage renown that Gladys had chosen to forego. They included Marek Jablonski, Jane Coop, Constance Channon Douglass, and Minuetta Shumiatcher-Kessler. Marilyn Engle followed in Gladys's footsteps by coming back to teach in Calgary after she had won major competitions in Canada and the United States and had toured North America as a concert pianist. "I've had offers to go to well-known places but I feel a strong bond with this city and I like the concept of continuity," said Engle. "To forget the past is a terrible loss."

Though widely recognized for her teaching ability—a visiting British adjudicator at the Calgary Music Festival described her as "one of the world's best music teachers"—Gladys never stopped studying and learning. Her students recalled, with some wonder, that when Gladys was sixty-nine she cancelled all lessons for two weeks. She went to New York to study with a young Juilliard teacher, who was said to be able to fix the technical problems that sometimes occur in the playing when a pianist is overworked or stressed. "Mrs. Egbert had decided that there existed someone who could give her new perspectives on the mysteries of piano performance," said Engle.

At the time of her death at age seventy-one, Gladys was still giving lessons to students from Drumheller to Lethbridge who travelled weekly to Calgary for their classes. Gladys returned the favour by attending their recitals when they made their debuts in their hometowns.

At her funeral, the presiding pastor said a eulogy would be redundant. Gladys had made Calgary the home of some of Canada's top pianists, and their playing on the concert stages of the world was a testament to the musical values she had promoted and instilled. A Calgary elementary school and the top prize at Calgary's annual Kiwanis Music Festival are named in her memory.

Lizzie Rummel

Mountaineer and environmentalist

1897–1980

Lizzie Rummel was a German-born baroness who fell in love with the Rocky Mountains as a child, while vacationing with her mother. She eventually made the mountain wilderness the focus of her life and work. For more than thirty years she ran lodges in the backcountry of the Rockies, became an authority on local flora and fauna, and was a friend to hundreds of hikers.

Born Elisabet von Rummel in Munich, she came to Canada in 1911 when her wealthy, travel-loving mother, Elsa Basilici, bought some ranch property in the Alberta foothills, sight unseen. The land was owned by a family friend in Munich, who charmed Elsa with his stories of the romance of the Canadian West. Daughter Elisabet, who inherited her aristocratic title from her father, a Bavarian army officer and actor named Baron Gustav von Rummel, was fourteen when she, her two younger sisters, and their mother spent their first summer on the ranch, located twenty miles southwest of Priddis.

The mother, who had married an Italian painter named Robert Basilici after divorcing Baron von Rummel, bought the Alberta ranch strictly for summer pleasure. She knew nothing about ranching. An English-born riding instructor named George Welsh looked after the horses and ranch chores, and a maid named Anna took care of the cooking and cleaning.

The family's comfortable situation changed dramatically in the summer of 1914 when war erupted throughout Europe. Elsa, Robert, and the three children found themselves stuck on the ranch, without passage to Germany and unable to get their money from home. The pleasure ranch became a working ranch. Robert had to learn about horses, and Elsa and her daughters had to learn about cooking and cleaning. It was a painful adjustment for a family used to living luxuriously with servants for every household task.

By the time the First World War was over, the ranch and foothills country of Alberta had become home for Elisabet and her two sisters. A trip back to Germany in 1919 convinced them that they never wanted to live there again. Their mother, who did want to stay in Europe, relented. In 1920, she returned to Alberta with her three daughters, but her husband Robert remained in Europe.

The girls, now in their twenties and all physically strong, did all the hard work on the ranch from breaking horses to raising milk cows. Elisabet, known to the family as Liesel or Lisi, also did the cooking and cleaning. For recreation they created their own home theatre, swam in the creek, went dancing at the Millarville community hall, listened at home to recordings of classical music, and read books from the three-hundred-volume library their mother shipped over from Germany.

Elisabet, who anglicized her first name to Elizabeth and dropped the aristocratic "von" from her last name, expanded her farm interests to include raising chickens, and won many awards at agricultural shows in Millarville and Calgary for her prize brown Leghorns.

By 1936, at age thirty-nine, Elizabeth was ready for a change. Her sisters were busy with their own lives after marrying local ranchers, and her mother was spending most of her time in New York living with friends. Elizabeth moved to Banff and then southwest to Mount Assiniboine to work as chambermaid, hostess, and mountain guide at a lodge owned by a man named Erling Strom. She didn't tell anyone she was a baroness. She preferred to be known simply as Lizzie Rummel.

Lizzie spent three summers working at Mount Assiniboine and spent her winters in Banff, where she worked in the hotel business and practised her skiing at nearby Mount Norquay. She also took up mountain climbing during this period. By 1942, she was a full-fledged member of the Alpine Club. In 1943, she became the manager of Skoki Lodge in the mountains just northeast of Lake Louise.

She managed the Skoki Lodge for seven years and simultaneously managed the nearby Temple Chalet and Lake Louise Ski Lodge. Whenever time permitted, she also worked as a ski guide. She barely broke even financially, but she loved the life. Comments in her guest books attest to her skill and popularity. "Many thanks to a perfect hostess," said one. "Food like this takes not only art, but genius," said another.

In 1950, at age fifty-four, Lizzie decided to buy her own mountain lodge on the shores of Sunburst Lake at Mount Assiniboine. Her friends told her she was crazy, but for more than a decade she had dreamed of having her own summer tourist camp in the mountains. This was the beginning of what she would later call "twenty beautiful years" of laughter and hard work, and hundreds of new and lasting friendships.

At first she did all the work herself, but as she got older she developed arthritis in her hip and had to hire a young woman to do the heavier work. She also had some help from a couple of male friends who cut wood and did odd jobs around the camp.

Her guests from around the world found the place idyllic and Lizzie to be the ideal mistress of the mountains. In her presence, they experienced a deeper appreciation of the beauty and wonder of the Rockies. "The person and the place are inseparable," wrote one visitor in her guest book. "It is part of my life to be here," wrote another. The guests were also impressed by her knowledge of mountain plants, flowers, and trails. She didn't attract enough visitors at first to support herself during the remainder of the year, so Lizzie spent her winters in Vancouver, working behind the counter in a coffee shop.

In 1959, Lizzie spent five months in a Calgary hospital recovering from hip surgery. That meant no summer at Assiniboine, but two friends stepped in to run Sunburst Camp for her. The following summer, Lizzie was back at Sunburst, using a cane but still able to do the work. By that time she no longer had to work in Vancouver in the off-season. She spent her winters in Banff, living in a log cabin that used to be the clubhouse of the Banff Curling Club.

For many of her guests, visiting with Lizzie was an important part of the experience of being in the mountains where silence is deafening, time expansive, and physical effort its own reward. "When you walked through the door," remembered one, "Lizzie made you feel like you were just the person she wanted to see."

Lizzie continued to spend her summers at Sunburst Lake until 1970 when she retired and sold the camp to the British Columbia government, which subsequently ran it as a boys' youth camp. Still she wasn't ready for retirement, as it turned out. In 1971, she worked as manager at the Castle Mountain youth hostel west of Banff. The following year, she worked as hostess at Strom Lodge near Mount Assiniboine where she had first started working when she left the ranch in the 1930s. The year after that, 1973, she made a trip to the Canadian Arctic at age seventy-six. She told friends her adventures weren't over yet. At age eighty, she flew into the mountains in a helicopter.

In April 1980, Lizzie received the Order of Canada. "She has enriched her country by sharing her deep love of the Rocky Mountains with all who meet her," said the citation. She died a few months later at age eighty-three. A school in Canmore and a lake in Kananaskis Country are named after her.

Norma Piper Pocaterra

Opera singer

1898–1983

In 1938, a Canadian opera singer using the stage name Norma San Giorgio was atop the European music world, hailed by critics in Milan as one of the best coloratura sopranos then singing on the Italian stage. A year later, her singing career was in ruins, interrupted by war and never to be revived. Her dream of international fame ended back where it began, in the churches and recital halls of Calgary.

She was a late bloomer as a singer. Born Norma Piper in Leamington, Ontario, she came to Calgary at age twenty when her mother died and her father, a dentist, decided to move the family west. She discovered she had a talent for singing when a Swiss-born opera star named Rudolph Brandli de Bevec came to town, and her father encouraged her to audition. De Bevec declared her a "natural" and said he would stay to give her lessons. By then, Piper was in her late twenties, somewhat old to be starting a music career but nevertheless determined to do so.

De Bevec moved to Vancouver in 1929, when his French-born wife said she could no longer stand living in Calgary. Norma followed him because she didn't want to stop her lessons. At age thirty-two she made her singing debut in Vancouver, performing at a charity show and drawing favourable reviews. Encouraged by her success, her father arranged for her to make her Calgary debut in 1931 at a recital in Central United Church. There, too, she attracted positive reviews. "All the bouquets that I got," she said. "It looked just like a funeral."

Over the next few years, Piper continued to gather good reviews as she performed in Western Canadian and American cities in concerts sponsored by local service clubs. She also sang on CBC Radio as an official staff soloist based in Vancouver.

In 1934, Piper went to Italy to further her training and make a career in grand opera. She carried a letter of introduction from Prime Minister R. B. Bennett—a friend of her father's—to the Canadian Trade Commissioner in Italy. His office helped her find accommodation in Milan but she had no luck finding a teacher who could prepare her for a career in opera. She was just on the verge of leaving Milan and trying her luck in London when George Pocaterra came into her life and turned her fortunes around.

Pocaterra was the son of a wealthy Italian industrialist and he had lived in Alberta for thirty years, owning and operating the Buffalo Head Guest Ranch on the banks of the Highwood River south of Calgary. When his father died in 1933, Pocaterra sold the ranch and returned to Italy to settle the estate. He carried with him a letter of introduction to Norma from a mutual friend in Calgary.

Pocaterra, through his influence and connections, opened doors for Norma that had previously been closed to her. He arranged for her to study with a top-class singing teacher, and he introduced her to some of the important people in Milan's music circles. Canada had been good to him, he said, and he wanted to return the favour by helping a Canadian do well in Italy.

Norma delayed her Italian debut for more than a year. "If I sing only well, I am one of a great crowd," she explained. She wanted to be acclaimed as the greatest soprano Canada had ever produced. A mediocre debut in Italy could destroy her chances of future success elsewhere. She wanted to make her name in Italy and eventually return to North America with an established reputation.

Her 1935 concert debut in Bergamo was less than a stunning success. A younger and more attractive soprano stole some of the limelight from her, but the performance did lead to a few low-paying engagements in small theatres. When she married Pocaterra, who had been acting as her business manager and financial supporter, her career took an upward swing. The marriage effectively stilled all gossip about their private lives and boosted her standing in Italian society. On stage she became Norma San Giorgio, assuming George's first name as her surname.

A successful 1937 concert tour of northern Italian cities paved the way for future triumphs. By the summer of 1939, Norma had lined up forty thousand dollars worth of concert engagements and a successful international career beckoned. However, the world had other plans.

War erupted. Norma and George abandoned Italy, said farewell to the operatic career that might have been, and made their escape to North America. They were not allowed to take money with them so they had to cable an American friend for help.

They spent several months in New York and Chicago trying to break into the American concert and opera circuit, but to no avail. Norma by then was in her forties and an unknown quantity in the United States. She was also unable to re-establish herself with the CBC. The producers told her that musical tastes had changed and that her dramatic singing style was no longer suitable for radio. The Pocaterras came back to Alberta to live in what they called "idyllic seclusion and genteel poverty" in a rented cabin located across the Highwood River from George's old Buffalo Head Guest Ranch. After a year, they settled on their own property near the Ghost River west of Calgary.

Calgary benefited enormously from Norma and George's decision to return to southern Alberta. In 1942, Norma joined Mount Royal College as a singing teacher and established herself as one of the city's top vocal coaches. George, who had spent his early years in Alberta exploring in the Kananaskis region, became active in local history circles and wrote articles for the newspapers. He also assisted on movie productions shot in nearby ranch country.

In 1955, the couple sold their Ghost Lake property and moved to a house in Calgary's Richmond Park. Norma retired from the College and began giving private lessons at her home. She was a fervent supporter of the arts and an enthusiastic booster of what is now the Calgary Opera.

George died in 1972. Norma continued giving private voice lessons and made it her crowd-pleasing practice to sing one of the big arias from her grand opera days at every one of her student recitals. She died in July 1983 at age eighty-five. She had some regrets, she said, over the wartime disruption of her operatic career, but she was not bitter. She had gone from early singing lessons in Calgary to grand opera in Italy in less than twelve years and that was reward enough.

Annora Brown

Artist

1899–1987

Annora Brown was a true trailblazer in a province that prides itself on its "can-do" spirit. She was one of the first Alberta-born artists to pursue a full-time professional career in the province as a painter. She was a founding member and the only female among the original members of the Alberta Society of Artists. She was also among the first Alberta painters to exhibit at the National Gallery in Ottawa.

Her life began—or, as she said, her *real* life began—on a day in 1925 when she first stepped across the threshold of the Ontario College of Art in Toronto to satisfy a gnawing desire to paint. A long and what she called "somewhat meaningless" period had preceded this. She had been through conventional high school in Fort Macleod, Alberta, with its mathematics, languages, and sciences— but no art. Even before she had a chance to write her final high-school exams, Annora was signed up to help the local school authorities deal with a drastic teacher shortage in rural Alberta.

She taught for four years, just long enough to realize that teaching would never become her vocation. Painting was her true calling. Many years before, her schoolteacher mother, who in Annora's words "was interested in things other than housework and gossip," had taken some painting lessons from a prominent Canadian artist of the period named Florence Carlyle. Her mother passed on what she had learned to Annora and that sowed the seeds.

An invitation to visit an aunt in Toronto opened the door of opportunity. What was to be a three-month visit turned into four years of study at the Ontario College of Art, where Annora's teachers included Arthur Lismer and J. E. H. MacDonald of the Group of Seven. Scholarships allowed Annora to complete the program. She returned to Alberta in 1929, full of ideas, and looking forward to making a living as an art instructor at Mount Royal College in Calgary.

At the end of her first year in Calgary, Annora's father phoned from the family farm in Fort Macleod to say that her mother had suffered a stroke. Could Annora come home to help out? Her heart sank at the thought. "I had been trained as a teacher and an artist, not as a nurse and a housekeeper. No need to dwell upon the difficulties of changing occupation and outlook." Refusing to let go of everything she had gained as an art student and teacher, she mentally divided herself: "Me" did the household chores and "Myself" painted and dreamed. She resolved to go outdoors every day and paint. "Only below-zero weather, a cloudburst, a hurricane, or a temperature of ninety degrees in the shade excused me."

Her aim as an artist was to celebrate what she saw as the untamed beauty of Alberta's "back yard." Well-meaning neighbours suggested that she might sell some of her paintings, if she painted pretty pictures of sailboats and windmills, but Annora was headed in a different direction. She wanted to paint grain elevators, dust storms, prairie trails, gophers, and wildflowers. "Being imprisoned in my own back yard, I set about trying to see it in depth."

Selling her paintings became secondary to the task of documenting the prairie landscape. "Once the habit of working, seeing, thinking is established, the artist never stops painting." The express delivery man became a regular visitor to her door, picking up crates of paintings that she submitted to various Canadian galleries for possible exhibition. Soon she was being recognized across Canada as a credible painter of the western scene. "In return for my efforts, I usually received a card of acceptance and a catalogue with my name in it."

After two years of painting to satisfy her needs as an artist, Annora started to paint for money. Her ailing father's life savings had dwindled because of her mother's medical bills and household expenses. She had to turn her talents in a commercial direction to support her father and herself. She began producing miniature paintings of wildflowers mounted on black mats that she sold at a dollar apiece as "handy and inexpensive gifts." She considered this to be tedious, potboiler work, but she consoled herself by noting that occasionally it brought someone to the house who went away with a larger painting.

During the 1940s, Annora expanded her commercial activity to include book illustrations, wall hangings, and handicraft designs. "Always in the back of my mind was the knowledge that while salaried workers were assured of a pension, the self-employed worker must provide his own." One commission was the front-page masthead for the *Fort Macleod Gazette*. She also taught community art classes for the University of Alberta extension department, and tried her hand at writing. Her book *Old Man's Garden*—named after the Native god said to have created her part of the world—is considered one of the best books ever written about southern Alberta's wildflowers.

Annora's father died in 1956 and afterward she began to take stock. Making an income from art was still a struggle for her, living in a small town, far away from galleries, city audiences, and art collectors. She began to concentrate on creating paintings of wildflowers that were small enough "to appeal to the pocketbooks of people living in a world where money had not yet lost its value." This work received a terrific boost when Calgary's Glenbow Museum commissioned her to produce no less than two hundred watercolours of different Alberta flowers.

In 1965, Annora left Fort Macleod and moved to a new home in Sidney, British Columbia. She needed, she said, to find "another hill." Success had created limitations and seemed to indicate an end to striving. "After arriving at the pinnacle there was nowhere else to go but down." Plus, she said, "My aging bones hoped for a milder climate." On the Saanich Peninsula, she found herself in the "company of people with interests similar to mine." She lived in a community of artists, many of them from Alberta. "We all talk of Alberta a lot and are all loyal," she said. She died in 1987 in her eighty-eighth year.

Llewellyn May Jones

Engineer and historian

1899–1986

Llewellyn May Jones was like many older Albertans during the last part of the twentieth century. Not only did she live a long life, but also she lived a most productive life. A lifelong learner, she achieved one educational first at age twenty-one when she became one of the first females in Canada to graduate from university with an engineering degree. She made the news again at age seventy-nine when she was awarded a master's degree in history at the University of Calgary.

Engineering was part of May's family tradition. One of her ancestors was George Stephenson, the Scotsman who oversaw the building of The Rocket, England's first steam locomotive. Her father was an engineer for a coal mining company in Springhill, Nova Scotia, where May was raised. His job sparked her interest in mathematical calculations and all things mechanical. "Father talked to me a lot, maybe because I was the youngest."

She graduated from the University of King's College in Halifax in 1920 and landed what was supposed to be an engineering job with a large mining corporation. "But they didn't want an engineer, they wanted a Girl Friday. Poor father almost had a fit when I told him I turned the job down."

Unable to find anything that would allow her to do what she called "real engineering," May returned to university, completed an education degree, and then headed west to take a teaching job at Calgary's Mount Royal College (MRC), then a Methodist-run boarding academy for high school students. "When I told father I was going to Alberta, and that I'd get a job once I got there, he didn't take that one too well either."

May taught math and science at MRC for two years. During that time she became engaged to Sidney Jones, a fellow Maritimer who had also been a King's College graduate unable to find work as an engineer. He taught math at Red Deer High School, and the two conducted a long-distance romance with weekend train travel until they married in 1923. Sidney landed a teaching job at Calgary's Central Collegiate Institute, and May left teaching to become a full-time homemaker and mother. In time, her son Don would follow in his parents' footsteps and become an engineer also.

During the Second World War, May finally had an opportunity to put her engineering training to good use. With a shortage of engineers left in Calgary to oversee the developing oil industry, May joined what is now the Alberta Energy and Utilities Board as assistant to the head geologist. "Some of the men wondered what on earth a woman was doing as an engineer," she said, "but I never stopped to think of myself as being a woman at that particular job. I just happened to fit into the picture at that time."

May did most of her wartime work in the oilfields of Turner Valley, and she acquired an intimate knowledge of the oil and gas business in Alberta. When the war was over she resigned. "One of the returning servicemen might need the job," she explained.

During the 1950s, May pursued an active career as a volunteer with the Mount Royal College Education Club, the Calgary Philharmonic, and the Engineering Institute of Canada. She co-founded the Calgary University Women's Club and was part of a group that lobbied successfully to have a branch of the University of Alberta established in Calgary.

May's husband died of a heart attack in 1971 when the two were on a visit back to Springhill. After she returned to Calgary, May decided in her mid-seventies to fulfil a longtime ambition and pursue a master's degree in history. Her thesis would be titled "The Search for Hydrocarbons: Petroleum and Natural Gas in Western Canada, 1883–1947." "I knew exactly what I wanted to write about," she said. "Good heavens, I was there for a lot of it."

Academics and oilpatch professionals welcomed publication of her thesis because it dealt with a period for which there was very little existing research. Much of her thesis was based on interviews with people who worked in the Alberta oil industry during the early years of exploration and development, and on her own experiences working in the industry during the Second World War. "It would be nice if it were useful for others," she said.

May didn't stop there. In her eighties, she wrote a sequel covering the period from 1947 to 1978, and she produced an exhibit on oil and gas history for what is now the Canadian Museum of Civilization in Ottawa. She mused about continuing with her university studies and earning a Ph.D. "That should keep me busy," she said.

Llewellyn May Jones died in September 1986 at age eighty-seven. "A pathfinder in the career of life, she found opportunity at every roadblock," wrote the late journalist Eva Reid, another standard-bearer for active old age in Alberta. Reid wrote a column for the old *Calgary Albertan* newspaper until she was seventy-three, retiring in 1980 only because the *Toronto Sun* bought the paper.

Clennell Haggerston "Punch" Dickins

Bush pilot

1899–1995

Prior to the 1920s, much of Canada's North was inaccessible in winter to southern dwellers and regarded as little more than an ice-covered frontier for future generations to explore. Then along came Punch Dickins and his fellow bush pilots to push back the frontier and establish regular air links with the south. In the process, they made commercial development possible and ensured that the aircraft became a familiar sight for northern residents who had never even seen a car or train.

Dickins was a pilot by the time he was eighteen. Born in Portage la Prairie, Manitoba, he was almost five years old in December 1903 when Orville and Wilbur Wright made the first heavier-than-air flight at Kitty Hawk, North Carolina. His family nicknamed him "Punch" because his older brother could not manage his first name, Clennell. From an early age, Punch showed a keen interest in flying machines.

When young Punch was eight, he moved with his family to Edmonton where his father worked in banking, insurance, and real estate. At age seventeen, Punch enrolled in mechanical engineering at the University of Alberta but left in his second year to join the Canadian infantry. After his battalion was sent to England, he transferred first to the Royal Flying Corps as a trainee pilot and then to its successor, the Royal Air Force. He was posted to a bomber and reconnaissance squadron operating over Flanders. Although seven victories were attributed to him in the course of seventy-six bombing raids, he claimed, with characteristic modesty, that his navigator was an excellent gunner. Nevertheless, he was awarded the Distinguished Flying Cross for gallantry.

He never told anyone but his wife, Constance, why he received the Distinguished Flying Cross. "The war is over," was all he would say to reporters. They managed to discover, however, that Dickins's squadron successfully bombed a German submarine base in Belgium where three other squadrons had failed.

After the war, Dickins worked briefly for General Motors in Edmonton, did some barnstorming, and played football for a year with the Edmonton Eskimos. When the Royal Canadian Air Force (RCAF) was created in 1924, he became one of the original officers. He carried out high-altitude experimental fighter flights over Edmonton and did forest patrol work out of High River. He also made aerial photographic surveys of northern Alberta and Saskatchewan, and tested new RCAF aircraft in winter conditions.

Aviation enthusiasts wanted to see regular airmail service established throughout the Canadian West after Lethbridge fliers Jock Palmer and Harry Fitzsimmons attempted the first airmail run from Lethbridge to Ottawa in June 1922. First someone had to find out if those early aircraft engines could function in subzero conditions. Dickins became a familiar sight around Edmonton, taking to the air in goggles, parka, high boots, and fur helmet, learning the hard way that a pilot could only stay warm by installing heaters in the cockpit.

He persuaded Edmonton's city engineer to clear a one-hundred-yard strip of willows and poplar trees on municipally owned land so that "we could land without having to worry about taking corners." When Blatchford Field opened for business in January 1927, Edmonton became the first city in Canada to have a municipal airport.

Dickins joined the newly formed Western Canada Airways in 1927 and flew the first aircraft on the prairie airmail circuit from Winnipeg to Regina, Calgary, and Edmonton, and back to Winnipeg. Over the next decade he was internationally celebrated for a series of pioneering flights over more than one million previously uncharted miles. He made the first flight across the unmapped Barren Lands of the Northwest Territories, and in 1929, became the first pilot to fly the two-thousand-mile length of the Mackenzie River, beginning his flight at Edmonton and touching down at Aklavik near the Beaufort Sea. He also made the first landing at Great Bear Lake where his passenger, the prospector Gilbert LaBine, started the first uranium mine. Perhaps his greatest achievement was a successful air survey to photograph blind spots along the Yukon-Northwest Territories border in 1935, a survey that truly opened up the Arctic.

His achievements earned him such nicknames as "The Snow Eagle" and "Canada's Sky Explorer," and stories of his stunts abounded in Edmonton. One had him flying a plane under Edmonton's High Level Bridge, a story Dickins would neither confirm nor deny. A man of few words, he preferred to let others do the talking. It was said the only speech he ever gave was his reply to the toast to the bride when he married Constance Gerrie in 1927.

In 1928, Dickins received the McKee Trophy for outstanding achievement in Canadian aviation, and in 1936, he received the Order of the British Empire. He wouldn't talk about those either, but every northerner knew the reason for the recognition. His flight across the trackless Barren Lands from Fort Smith to Baker Lake had been as much a trail-blazing effort as the construction of the Canadian Pacific Railway's main line.

As a pilot, Dickins was both daring and cautious. He believed flying was safe if planes were properly inspected, which he did before every flight. He heeded bad weather signs and used common sense. Although he didn't take foolish risks, he sometimes depended on luck to get him out of tough spots. The only time he ran out of aviation fuel in the North he landed on the banks of the Slave River. He didn't have a radio and was trying to build a raft when a paddle-wheeler pulled up alongside him. The skipper said that he did have some aircraft fuel aboard. He was keeping twenty-five barrels of it "for some guy named Dickins who thinks he is going to fly in here next winter."

In 1941, Britain's minister of aircraft production—Canadian-born Lord Beaverbrook—called in Dickins, who was then assistant to the president of Canadian Pacific Airlines, and asked him to become operations manager of Atfero, the air ferry organization that flew desperately needed American-built bombers across the Atlantic. Dickins had built up transatlantic deliveries of 150 aircraft a month by the time the organization was turned over to RAF Ferry Command in 1942.

Dickins then became general manager of Canadian Pacific Airlines with a mandate to amalgamate a number of small and scattered airlines into one network. At the same time he oversaw the management of six flying schools that trained twelve thousand aircrew in Canada as part of the British Commonwealth Air Training Plan.

The federal government's creation of Trans-Canada Airlines before the war meant that the growth potential for Canadian Pacific Airlines was restricted after the war and in 1947 Dickins became vice-president in charge of sales for de Havilland of Canada. For twenty years he played an important part in marketing the five-seater Beaver, still a standard plane for northern flying, and the twin-engine Otter, to more than sixty countries.

In 1973, after he retired, Dickins was named a member of Canada's Aviation Hall of Fame. His citation read: "Despite adversity, he dramatized to the world the value of the bush pilot, and his total contribution to the brilliance of Canada's air age can be measured not only by the regard in which he is held by his peers, but by the nation as a whole."

Dickins spent the first years of his retirement living in Victoria, compiling material for a history of Canadian aviation. He gave up his pilot's licence at age seventy-eight ("I had it for sixty years," he lamented) and spent his final years in a Toronto retirement home where he died in 1995 at age ninety-six. Shortly before his death he asked Constance if they could return home. By that he meant Edmonton, where he and Constance had met and where he built their first house. The Edmonton neighbourhood of Dickinsfield is named after him, as is Lake Dickins in northwestern Alberta.

Frank McMahon

Industrialist

1902–1986

Luck and tenacity have always been the defining qualities of the gamblers who make it big in the oil business, and Frank McMahon had these qualities in abundance. Born in the small mining town of Moyie, British Columbia, he rose from modest beginnings to become one of the biggest players in the history of the Canadian petroleum industry.

His father was a drifter from Barkerville, British Columbia, who abandoned his wife and three sons when the boys were just children. Frank, the oldest, attended high school in Kimberley, British Columbia, and college in Spokane, Washington, where he studied business administration.

McMahon left Spokane in his third year and headed south to make his fortune. He worked as a labourer on the construction of the Golden Gate Bridge in San Francisco, and then worked as a diamond driller and gas explorer in various parts of the United States, Canada, and Mexico.

In 1936, a major oil strike in Turner Valley prompted McMahon to set up an oil drilling company, West Turner Petroleums, which he ran with his brothers George and John. For two years, the company brought in nothing but dirt. Undeterred, Frank put up his last one hundred dollars in cash to obtain a land option near where oil had already been found, borrowed twenty thousand dollars more to purchase the eighty-acre lease, resumed drilling, and struck black gold to the tune of thirty-five hundred barrels a day.

For the next eight years, McMahon struggled. He merged West Turner with another leaseholder, British Pacific Oils, to form Pacific Petroleums, a company that would eventually become one of Canada's largest independent oil and gas producers. It wasn't until 1948, however, the year after the historic Imperial Oil strike at Leduc, that McMahon began to move into the big leagues. He drilled two wells in Leduc that came in normally as conventional oil producers, and a third, named Atlantic No. 3, that made his fortune. It was a rogue well that gushed out of control for six months, spewed out ten thousand barrels of oil and one hundred million cubic feet of natural gas daily, created a forty-acre lake of oil, and then caught fire. Others might have despaired but not McMahon. He recovered most of the spilled oil, shipped it to market, and made his first million-dollar profit.

After that, McMahon never looked back. The well-publicized blaze had proven he could find oil and gas. As a result, he had no trouble attracting international investment money. He found a major source of natural gas in the Peace River area of northwestern Alberta, and that posed a new challenge for him because he needed a pipeline to get the gas to markets in Vancouver and the northwestern United States. With characteristic determination, he spent the next decade battling government regulators and American rivals to establish Westcoast Transmission as Canada's first major gas pipeline.

During the 1950s and 1960s, McMahon was regularly in the news. He was referred to variously as a flamboyant oil tycoon with an estimated worth of fifty million dollars, as a hard-drinking wheeler-dealer who boasted "there's one thing strong going for us in Washington, and that's our breath," as a champion racehorse owner, and as a backer of hit Broadway musicals.

In 1960, he and brother George put up three hundred thousand dollars of the one million dollars needed to build a new football park in Calgary. It was named McMahon Stadium, and it became the home of the Canadian Football League's Calgary Stampeders. Frank's other sporting interest, horse racing, brought him winners on both sides of the Atlantic. With Bing Crosby (a former classmate in Spokane) and newspaper tycoon Max Bell, he owned Meadow Court, a winner of the Irish Derby, the Epsom Derby, and the King George VI and Queen Elizabeth Stakes. Bought for nine thousand dollars, the horse was eventually put out to stud for total fees of $1.26 million. McMahon also owned a horse that won both the Kentucky Derby and the Preakness.

As a member of the Canadian corporate establishment, McMahon sat on the board of the Royal Bank and belonged to

Montreal's exclusive Mount Royal Club. His homes included a mansion in Vancouver, a resort property in Palm Beach, a tax haven in Bermuda, and an apartment in New York. While in New York, he invested successfully in such shows as *The Pajama Game* and *Damn Yankees*, as well as backing a few flops. That led him to advise other potential Broadway investors to "put lots of money into the good ones and not much into the bad ones."

From the late 1960s onward, McMahon had little connection with the Alberta oil business. He gave up control of Pacific Petroleums when Phillips Petroleum of Oklahoma became a major partner in the enterprise, and he began to spend more and more time in Bermuda where he died in 1986, a casualty of emphysema and gin. "Characters of previous ages sometimes tend to grow in stature as they recede into history," observed author Peter Foster, "but there is little doubt that Frank McMahon was a giant among oilmen."

Francis Winspear

Philanthropist

1903–1997

"You can't take it with you, so you should put what you leave behind to good use." That has been the philosophy of every community-minded Albertan who has made money in this province and then given some of it back. One of them was Francis Winspear, the most generous philanthropist and patron of the arts that Edmonton has ever seen.

The son of a Birmingham shopkeeper who immigrated to Canada with his family in 1910, young Francis grew up in a rural hamlet located between Strathmore and Gleichen. His father ran a general store while doubling as postmaster, secretary of the school board, justice of the peace, and a lay reader in the Anglican Church. The Winspear home was a haven for the young English immigrants who worked for the Canadian Pacific Railway constructing irrigation canals in the area. "They could drop in for dinner, and they knew they would always be welcome," said Winspear. "Many of them had very fine singing voices, many of them had good musical educations. I suppose ours was the only piano in twenty miles."

Winspear finished high school in Calgary and then worked as a bank clerk while taking a "banker's course" by correspondence from Queen's University in Kingston, Ontario. His fascination with accounting and economics led to a decision to be a chartered accountant. He articled in Calgary with Touche and Company, and then landed a job in the Edmonton office of Peat Marwick Mitchell.

In 1930, at age twenty-six, he decided to leave Peat Marwick Mitchell and strike out on his own. "I found I had the knack, first, of attracting new clients and, second, of finding things to do that chartered accountants didn't ordinarily do—such as advising lawyers on insurance claims. In a very short time I had more men working for me than they had in Calgary. Yet ours was still a suboffice, which I resented, so I decided that I'd better start my own practice."

Winspear set up his own Edmonton practice with a single client. He was in debt to the tune of $936.14, with no reserves. But at the end of the year his one-man practice had net income of more than four thousand dollars, and he had taken on his first articling student. Winspear said that the Depression actually created prospects for accountants with analytical skills who could help make businesses cost effective. "Sometimes we made frightful bloomers, but our successes far outnumbered our failures."

While building his practice, Winspear taught accounting part-time at the University of Alberta. The university asked him to do this, he said, because "accountancy lectures had floundered in a sea of alcohol." The regular instructor was prone to disappearing for several weeks on end due to problems with booze, and the university needed someone to fill in until a permanent replacement could be found. Winspear took the part-time position and kept the job for eighteen years. When he stopped instructing in 1948, he was a full professor and director of the university's School of Commerce. By that time, Winspear's practice had expanded into a major accounting firm with offices across Western Canada. It was also one of the leaders in the post-war transformation of the accounting firm into a business consulting firm.

As well as using his accounting skills to salvage struggling businesses, Winspear invested in and launched as many as forty business ventures of his own. They included such mainstays of the Alberta economy as Premier Steel, which opened the first steel plant in the province; Northwest Industries, an aircraft repair company; and Gold Standard Oils, which was a key player in the Great Canadian Oil Sands venture. Winspear also held a controlling interest in B.C. Airlines, Swanson Lumber, Echo Bay Mining, and Consolidated Finance. A sentimental favourite was Calgary-based Brock Western, a dry goods and textile distribution company that he bought from his father. "My father was an absolutely first-class salesman and merchandiser, but he had no idea whatsoever of finance." After turning the company around, Winspear transferred a block of shares to his father and put in place a company pension plan from which his father could benefit. "My father was able to live comfortably for the rest of his life."

Winspear retired from active involvement in business in 1964 at age sixty-one, and he devoted the rest of his life to philanthropy. "Finance is fun," he said. Giving, on the other hand, was serious business. "After one has attained some affluence, there remains the problem of how to use the money wisely," he wrote in an autobiography published in 1968. "Giving money requires even more prescience, more imagination, more executive skill than making it." As long as disease existed, and as long as Canadians thirsted for music, art, and swimming pools, the businessman could never really retire. "His talents are needed. He faces a continuous challenge."

His alma mater, the University of Alberta, became a major beneficiary of Winspear's generosity. University president Rod Fraser estimated that over a twenty-year period Winspear donated "at least" six million dollars to the faculties of business, arts, medicine, and education. Winspear also gave generously to the University of Victoria. President of the University of Victoria, David Strong, recalled receiving a phone call from the philanthropist when the university was trying to raise money for a public policy professorship. "Do you think one million dollars would be acceptable?" asked Winspear, and then promptly wrote out a cheque for that amount.

Winspear particularly enjoyed supporting musical activities because, for him, business and culture were inseparable. "I feel that music is part of an educated man's well-being," he said. "He thinks better. Did you ever notice how many top-flight mathematicians are also very good musicians?" He believed that a cultured society was a prosperous society. He endowed the University of Alberta with the means to hire the conductor and concertmaster of the Edmonton Symphony as visiting professors, and he gave six million dollars toward construction of a new forty-five-million-dollar concert hall in Edmonton. That was one of the largest single contributions ever given to a performing arts centre in Canada. Normally, a gift of one million dollars is enough to ensure that an auditorium is named after the patron. "I've got to give enough money so that people will be almost shamed into coming along," said Winspear.

In 1995, media reports suggested that Winspear had a fortune of one hundred million dollars. However, he denied the reports. "That's far too generous," he said. "I've given most of it away." He agreed with a reporter's guess that he "only" had about twenty million dollars left. He said every businessman should give a fixed percentage of his income to support worthy causes. "He's got a responsibility to those who follow him to help make a contribution to civilization."

Along with giving away his money, Winspear tried later in life to change Canada's political structure for the better. A lifelong federal Liberal Party supporter who worked as a fundraiser in Alberta for the party under Lester Pearson, Winspear became disillusioned with what he felt was the Trudeau government's fiscal irresponsibility in the 1970s. He supported the Mulroney Tories for a while, but they didn't do the job for him either. He concluded that Canada needed a new political voice and new leadership. In 1985, he gathered a group of like-minded individuals at his summer home on Vancouver Island's Saanich Peninsula, and put together the framework and the financial backing for what became the Reform Party of Canada, now the Canadian Alliance Party. "It always irritated me that the government of Canada has been repeatedly dominated by southern Ontario and Quebec," said Winspear.

Winspear died at age ninety-three in January 1997, eight months short of seeing his dream for a concert hall in Edmonton materialize as a finished product. Seventeen years in the planning and construction, the Francis Winspear Centre for Music finally opened in September 1997, and was hailed by musicians, critics, and audience members as being acoustically superb. "He knew it was going to be good," acknowledged his wife, Harriet Winspear. "The best hall in North America. That's really something for Edmonton to have."

Catharine Robb Whyte

Painter and philanthropist

1906–1979

There are museums of local history and culture across Canada but few do better than Banff's Whyte Museum of the Canadian Rockies in explaining who lived in this part of the world, what they did, and how they shaped the region as it now exists. The Whyte Museum reveals that Banff is not just another resort town with motels, tour buses, and souvenir shops but that it is a key to the Rocky Mountains. It shows that the mountains, in turn, are a part of the essential Canadian experience of standing alone in the face of untamed nature. Since the 1880s, Banff has attracted hikers, climbers, skiers, and nature lovers from around the world, and they have left a collective record of their wanderings and explorations in the Rockies. That record is what gives the Whyte Museum its sense of purpose and belonging.

The museum exists because of the generosity of Catharine Robb Whyte, a wealthy New England heiress who lived in the Rockies for close to fifty years. She used her inheritance to create what she called a "place where the good, the wise and the beautiful come together in harmony."

Born in Concord, Massachusetts, Catharine was part of a family steeped in intellectual, artistic, and business traditions. Her maternal grandfather, Edward Sylvester Morse, was a Victorian intellectual, marine biologist, and the founding director of the Peabody Museum in Salem, Massachusetts. Her mother, Edith Morse Robb, made her living designing and producing needlepoint patterns. Her Iowa-born father, Russell Robb, was senior vice-president and treasurer of a large Boston engineering firm.

After attending private school in Providence, Rhode Island, where she was courted in her teens by John D. Rockefeller III, Catharine made her bow to Boston society at age eighteen. At her mother's encouragement, she then enrolled as a part-time art student at the School of the Museum of Fine Arts in Boston. "My mother wanted me to be an artist more than I did," she explained. She attended as a half-day student while deciding if she really wanted to pursue art as a career.

During her first year, she met Peter Whyte, a Banff storekeeper's son, attending on scholarship. He had little money and no social connections, but he did have a passion for art. He was strongly influenced by the painters Carl Rungius, Belmore Browne, and Nora Drummond-Davis, who had all lived in Banff. Catharine soon began to share that passion. "We are just a couple of crazy artists," she wrote in a letter to her mother. They were also in love. They married in 1930 and moved to Banff, where they would spend the rest of their lives.

For a short while in the 1930s, Catharine and Peter ran what is now the Skoki Lodge, northeast of Lake Louise. After that, most of their life was devoted to art, globetrotting, and the pleasures of the Rockies. Catharine's money made this possible. She had about a million dollars in her bank account when they married, and she inherited several million more in later years.

They did much of their painting in the Rockies, about an hour's hiking distance from their Banff studio-home. Catharine said that the Maine coastline she had loved as a child was dull and unexciting compared to the rugged beauty of the mountain landscape. "The changing light, the effects, they're always fascinating, and now I wouldn't live anywhere else." Sometimes she painted portraits, but the mountains were always her real subject.

Catharine and Peter didn't sell many of their paintings during the Great Depression, aside from a few that they sold to the tourists staying at the Banff Springs Hotel, but that didn't deter them from spending most of their time in the outdoors, drawing and painting. They loved the mountains and would have been pleased to know that some of the top climbers in the world still stop at the Whyte Museum to prepare for their ascents by studying the maps and charts in the museum's collection.

The Whytes started planning the museum during the 1950s. All their lives they had loved museums, archives, and collections of any kind. They were two of nature's packrats, and Catharine especially kept meticulous records of everything they did, saw, or thought. In that respect she was influenced by her grandfather Edward Morse, who had a passion for collecting, cataloguing, and exhibiting. Because she and Peter had postponed raising a family until it was too late, they decided Catharine's inherited millions should benefit the public, and they began imagining a museum that would preserve their ideals and their art.

In 1958, Catharine wrote to her mother about her ideas for a combined art gallery, library, and historical museum. She and Peter created a foundation to handle the details, and a medicine man from the nearby Stoney reserve gave them the name for the foundation: "Wa-Che-Yo-Cha-Pa" which he translated as, "Anything you see, anything you do, it's perfect." Later it became known simply as the Peter and Catharine Whyte Foundation.

The Whytes continued sketching and painting during the 1960s, but their output dwindled as Peter descended into alcoholism and Catharine devoted more and more of her time to recording and collecting historical material and correspondence for the new museum.

Peter died in December 1966 at age sixty-one. Eighteen months later, the mountain artists Jimmy Simpson and Charlie Beil were on hand to cut the buckskin thong and officially open the Philippe Delesalle-designed building that has become the centrepiece of the Whyte Museum. Today, the complex also includes two houses that Catharine left to the public. One is the ten-room log home the Whytes built and in which they lived together. The other is the home that belonged to Catharine's friends the Moores.

As she grew older, Catharine became widely recognized as a living link with Banff's past. She was a familiar figure in the town, often seen walking along Banff Avenue modestly dressed in inexpensive clothes that gave no hint of the riches she brought with her as a young bride. In her seventies, she was still the hiker she had been when she and Peter painted together in the mountains. She often walked up to a spot on Tunnel Mountain overlooking Banff. From there she could look down on the town in which she had lived for half a century, and in which she left a record of her life and times in one of the world's smallest yet most acclaimed international museums. She died in August 1979 at age seventy-two.

Eva Reid

Journalist

1907–1989

Eva Reid made her mark in Alberta journalism at a time when the role of women in the news business was largely restricted to mindlessly filling the social columns with throwaway items about weddings, tea dances, and the movements of the rich and influential. Reid did her share of society gossip columns in her day, but she also worked as a police court reporter, and that combination earned her the respect of her male colleagues. Where else would you find a reporter who knew as much about the Criminal Code as she did about Emily Post?

She entered journalism by accident. Born in Orangeville, Ontario, Reid was raised on a farm near Fort Macleod, went to high school in Calgary, studied business, and worked as a secretary before becoming involved with the emerging Social Credit movement of William "Bible Bill" Aberhart. During the early years of the Great Depression, Reid spent much of her spare time at Aberhart's Prophetic Bible Institute in Calgary, listening and learning. For a while she boarded in the Aberhart home. When she moved out, an Aberhart disciple and future premier named Ernest Manning moved in to take her room.

Reid became a staunch Social Credit supporter because "it appealed to my young mind." Whenever she visited her home in Fort Macleod, she would see all these young farmers who, "through no fault of their own, got caught up in the Depression. Social Credit seemed to have the answers."

Not everyone agreed that Social Credit had the answers. Many of the province's newspapers considered Aberhart's economic schemes—which included such proposals as paying a twenty-five-dollar monthly dividend to every Alberta citizen and printing the province's own money to combat the power of the Eastern Canadian banks—to be unsound, impractical, and unworkable. To counteract the negative publicity, Aberhart started his own newspaper, the *Social Credit*

Chronicle, and invited Reid to write columns for it. She happily complied, dutifully transcribing the political sermons of Aberhart and Manning, and writing stories about the impact of the depression on Alberta's farmers.

By 1935, the work of Aberhart, Manning, and the *Social Credit Chronicle* had paid off. Social Credit was in power. Two years later, its propagandist purpose having been served, the *Chronicle* was sold to George Bell, publisher of the *Calgary Albertan* newspaper. Reid was transferred to the *Albertan* as part of the transaction. Her days as an active political worker then ended, but she remained close to the Aberhart and Manning families. She was a guest at Manning's wedding when he married Prophetic Bible Institute organist Muriel Aileen Preston.

The *Chronicle* survived briefly as an insert in the *Albertan*, then quietly folded. Reid, then earning fourteen dollars a week, became provincial editor. She was one of the first women in Canada to hold such a position. Her job, as she described it, was to assemble the news "from Barrhead to the border" (the border being the Canada-United States boundary). Her correspondents phoned in stories about crimes and forest fires, and Reid remembered having to wait for some of the stringers to finish their fire-fighting duties for the day before they could call her with the news. She then hammered out the story on her Underwood typewriter to meet her late-night deadline.

During the Second World War, with international events engaging the attention of newspaper readers everywhere, provincial news was relegated to the back pages. Reid became the *Albertan's* women's editor and police court reporter; a double assignment necessitated by a shortage of men in the newsroom due to the war. It kept her busy from 10 A.M. until midnight daily. She spent her days at court, documenting the misdeeds of Calgary's felons. She then rushed back to the office to file her stories, changed into her evening gown, and headed off to cover the social events of the evening. Moving daily from the world of the seamy to the world of high society involved both a mental adjustment as well as a change of clothing. Reid never became cynical. She brought the same enthusiasm to breaking a story about the engagement of a prominent debutante as she did to covering a juicy murder or robbery.

As a reporter, she never balked at covering the bloodiest crime or traffic accident. She recalled one particularly horrendous accident, early in her newspaper career, when two vehicles collided on the Banff Coach Road and there were "arms and legs all over." An *Albertan* assignment editor decided Reid should cover the story to "see if I had any guts." She did.

Because of her social connections, she became the envy of other reporters in the newsroom. She rubbed shoulders with the Lougheeds and the Mannixes and knew them on a first-name basis. The reclusive industrialist Fred C. Mannix, who wouldn't speak to other reporters, was just "Freddy" to Eva Reid.

She gave up the police beat after the Second World War and carried on as women's editor. In 1961, she became one of the few women in Canada to have a regular city column in a daily newspaper. She covered the passing parade of local notables and chronicled such events as the building of the Calgary Tower and the opening of the first phase of the Calgary International Airport. She continued doing this job until 1980 when the *Toronto Sun* bought the *Albertan* and Reid, at age seventy-three, decided she needed a rest. She left without a pension because the *Albertan* had no pension plan in place when she started working there, but she had no words of bitterness about this. She knew she had been exploited, but she accepted this reality because she had loved being in the news business for the forty-five years she worked there. She died in 1989 at age eighty-two. Her friends held a big garage sale of her personal effects and used the proceeds to fund a journalism scholarship at Mount Royal College that is now administered through the Calgary Foundation.

Herman Linder

Rodeo cowboy champion

1907–2001

The trail to rodeo riches is littered with broken limbs and broken dreams. Herman Linder was one of the talented and lucky few who made it all the way to the end of the trail. He built a ranching spread in Cardston from the proceeds of one of the most successful careers in the history of Canadian rodeo.

The Linder name is prominent in the story of cowboy sport during the 1930s. Not only was Herman remarkably versatile, winning every event in the rodeo from bull riding to calf roping to steer decorating, but his older brother Warner also made a few championship moves of his own before deciding he preferred ranching to rodeo.

The brothers started riding before they were teenagers, clambering aboard wild steers and stray range horses on their father's farm near Cardston. "Anything that moved, we rode it," said Herman. They inherited their athletic ability from their father, a former circus acrobat and tightrope walker from Switzerland, who immigrated to North America at the turn of the century.

After running a cheese factory in Wisconsin, where Warner was born in 1906 and Herman was born in 1907, the elder Linder decided to move his family to southern Alberta where, according to the Canadian Pacific Railway advertisements, the land was cheap and the crops were rich. He settled just north of the American border and began to raise cattle and crops.

Herman began his rodeo career in an unusual and somewhat questionable way at age fourteen, appearing as a female bronc rider named "Alberta Pearl" in the Cardston rodeo of 1921. The organizers had advertised an appearance by a "girl bronc rider" and pulled off the stunt by paying Herman six dollars to ride a bucking horse wearing a wig and a dress. Herman said afterward that he felt like a fool and regretted the whole affair.

Two years after his forgettable debut as a "cowgirl," Herman entered a professional rodeo contest under his own name and won. He continued to win over the next sixteen years, capturing championships in four countries and three continents. "He blazed like a meteor across the rodeo skies," wrote his biographer, Harald Gunderson.

Herman credited his brother as being the better rider, but accident-prone. His horses "seemed to fall with him, run into things, or into or over fences that would result in severely bruised or broken bones." Warner still managed to find the winner's circle, despite his injuries. At the 1936 Calgary Stampede, he won both the North American steer decorating championship and the Canadian calf-roping championship with his back in a brace, his collarbone broken, and his ligaments torn. Herman scored two first-place finishes at the same rodeo, prompting the *Calgary Herald* to describe the brothers' achievement as "the greatest two-man show in the history of the Calgary Stampede."

Aside from winning championships, Herman was prominent as an advocate for the sport, helping organize the first association of rodeo cowboys to make the point that they were professional athletes and should be treated as such. They called themselves The United Cowboys Turtle Association not because cowboys were slow of body or mind, but because they were independent souls, slow to take group action.

Their first group action occurred at the Boston Gardens in 1936. Herman and sixty of his fellow cowboys went on strike for better working conditions. They noted that the prize money on offer wasn't much more than the entry fees, which meant the cowboys were risking their necks just to win back the money they paid to compete. They protested by attending the rodeo as paying customers and roundly booing the incompetent riders brought in as replacements. The organizers capitulated and gave the cowboys what they wanted. The cowboys later presented Herman with a plaque reading, "A turtle never got anywhere if he didn't stick his neck out."

Herman retired from rodeo competition in 1940, at age thirty-two. At that point, he was at the height of his fame, having won twenty-two championships at the Calgary Stampede—a record never equalled. Headline writers dubbed him "The Cowboy Supreme" and

"King of the Cowboys." Historian James H. Gray called him "everybody's choice for the all-time Canadian all-around cowboy."

He ended his career on a winning note at a rodeo in Lewiston, Idaho. "None of the boys ever thought I'd quit, but I had made up my mind." Linder had decided he would take his rodeo winnings and settle in Cardston with his wife, the former Agnes Zeller of South Dakota. They expanded the 750,000-acre cattle ranch he had bought with his earlier winnings, moved out of the little log cabin he and Agnes had called home for the first seven years of their itinerant marriage, and built the comfortable bungalow that would be his home for the rest of his life. "There was a time in life, time to quit," he said.

Quitting did not suit Linder initially. "That first winter, I just about wore the living room rug out pacing up and down," he said. "It finally struck me that, after ten years of steady riding on the rodeo circuit, my friends were all on the road." He returned to the circuit as a judge, then spent thirty years on the road as a rodeo producer. Agnes was his constant companion. The only time she missed a big event was when she faced a choice of getting a new cook stove or travelling to London with Herman to attend a three-week Wild West show. The stove won out.

Warner looked after the ranch while Herman was on the road. The arrangement worked fine as long as Herman was away. A certain edginess to the fraternal relationship, arising from Warner's style of ranch management, resulted in Warner finally leaving the spread to live in the town of Cardston. However, the brothers and their wives still got together regularly for card games.

Herman scored many successes as a rodeo promoter. Among them was his staging of The Great Western Rodeo at Montreal's Expo '67, which made money despite a transit strike and rain. He also had his share of reverses. One saw him convicted in a Vancouver police court in 1949 on a charge of maltreating a horse by using a pain-inflicting flank strap to make it buck. The B.C. Supreme Court eventually overturned the conviction. "A ruling like that should not be allowed to go unchallenged," said Linder. "It was an attack against the whole rodeo industry."

Linder retired from active rodeo in 1969 with enough plaques, belt buckles, trophy saddles, and hall-of-fame citations to turn his home into a rodeo museum. Among his many honours and awards was membership in six rodeo halls of fame and being named Cardston's male athlete of the century—a singular triumph in a town where high school basketball reigns supreme. At age ninety he was named to the Order of Canada. "He stands out as an individual who has contributed his time and energy to keep the province's rangeland heritage alive and flourishing," said the accompanying citation.

Herman died in January 2001 at age ninety-three. His second wife, the former Adeline Tellesch, an old family friend he married in 1990, five years after he lost Agnes to a brain tumour, survived him. Brother Warner predeceased him in 1983.

Betty Pedersen

Champion of farm women's rights

1908–1993

In June 2000, at an emotion-filled meeting in Wainwright, the Women of Unifarm voted to disband due to declining membership. Thus ended an eighty-five-year history of organized farm women in Alberta. It was a far cry from the days when rural women desperately needed the likes of Betty Pedersen and her social reformer colleagues to give voice to their concerns.

Pedersen served with the Alberta farm women's organization from the 1930s to the 1970s. She was a teacher by training and a feminist by disposition. Born Elizabeth Binnie in Edinburgh, Scotland, she came to Calgary with her family in 1912, when she was four years old. Her father worked in the cartage business and as a railway construction crew supervisor.

Betty graduated in 1926 from Calgary Normal School and taught in various Alberta communities until 1933 when she married Orla Pedersen, a Danish immigrant farmer. They farmed northeast of Strathmore near Standard. Betty continued to teach part-time and served her community as secretary of the Standard Community Hall Association, president of the Home and School Association, and as a Sunday school superintendent.

Betty considered herself to be an equal partner in both the work of the farm and the farm decision-making. She attended to the books and to various chores around the farmyard while raising her two children, cooking the meals, supporting her husband, and working for church and community. She packed water from the pump, fed the pigs, and nursed the calves. She was no different from many other farm women in assuming such responsibilities, yet she somehow felt that her role in the farm partnership was diminished by prevailing chauvinistic attitudes. It was a case, said Pedersen, of "You do your role and I do my role and you're still subservient to me."

The Women of Unifarm provided her with the means to work

for fairness, justice, and equity for farm women. Formed in 1915 as the Women's Auxiliary of the United Farmers of Alberta, the organization had evolved over the years from a social club for lonely and isolated farm women into a powerful lobby group. In the same way that male farmers became politically powerful through organizing, farm women began to feel their power when they came together and started working for the development and improvement of social, health, and education services for rural Albertans. They assumed responsibility for these issues because they were keenly interested in them, and because they knew they were not priorities for the men. "The men pretty well left it to them and said, 'that's women's work, now you do it,'" said Pedersen.

In the beginning, Pedersen faced the same kind of discrimination that earlier generations of farm women had experienced. She recalled attending an executive meeting of the men's organization when a director asked her, "What are you doing here? You should be home in your kitchen cooking your husband's supper." However, she was strong and determined, and not about to let such sarcastic remarks stop her from effecting change and helping people.

Pedersen achieved some of her greatest successes from the late 1960s to the mid-1970s when the organization evolved from the Farm Women's Union of Alberta into Women of Unifarm. Pedersen served as president during those years and worked for such causes as improved women's property rights and legal status, planned parenthood, and sex education in the schools. Almost single-handedly she was responsible for bringing family planning clinics into rural Alberta, and she lobbied persistently to have seniors' lodges established in the province. "Sometimes, to be truthful, we wondered at our own temerity as we delved into matters of education, health and all the social aspects of rural living," she said in a preface that she and former president Louise Johnston wrote for a history of the organization. The book, *Politics, Pitchforks and Pickle Jars: 75 Years of Organized Farm Women in Alberta*, written by Nanci Langford, was published in 1997, four years after Pedersen's death.

In 1975, Pedersen was a loud voice in the national outcry following the Irene Murdoch case. In the case, the Supreme Court of Canada ruled that a Turner Valley woman who had helped run the family ranch had done "just about what the ordinary rancher's wife does" and had no right to a share in it. Pedersen, who had organized additional legal assistance for Murdoch and instigated awareness and fundraising campaigns, saw to it that the issue of matrimonial property rights was once again put on the agendas of women's organizations. The ensuing protest produced reforms in provincial matrimonial property laws across Canada.

Pedersen sought no recognition for her involvement in women's causes but it came to her anyhow. In 1976, she became only the fifth woman since 1951 to be inducted into the Alberta Agriculture Hall of Fame. "She has become known as a person who gets things done," said the accompanying citation. Pedersen acknowledged that farm women had achieved many changes for the better because of their lobbying efforts. "As far as changing the laws are concerned, I think the women have done a great deal," she said. "They haven't done an outstanding job, but they have done better than the men have."

Rheumatoid arthritis and other health problems forced Pedersen to curtail her involvement in Women of Unifarm during the 1980s, but she did maintain an active association with the Goldeye Lake youth camp near Nordegg, which was established to develop leadership and citizenship in young Albertans. Pedersen predicted that leadership training for young people would become increasingly important as the family farm withstood the threats of big commercial and co-operative farming enterprises.

Pedersen died in 1993 at age eighty-four. Three years later, the Women of Unifarm voted for the first time on a motion to disband the organization. There were too few members left to sustain it and too many were in their senior years. The motion was defeated, but the writing was on the wall. Membership continued to decline over the next four years until Women of Unifarm finally folded in 2000. "This feels like sending grandma to the nursing home," said one member sadly.

Ernest Manning

Preacher and premier

1908–1996

On the seventh day, Ernest Manning preached, and that defined his style and substance as a political leader. Though he was always careful to keep his Sunday-side out of the Alberta legislature, he made no attempt to hide the fact that his Baptist faith shaped the fiscally conservative and socially reformist government he led for twenty-five years. It is hard to imagine today how fundamentalist religion and politics were ever so complementary.

A mail-order Philco radio that he purchased in 1924 set Manning on the career path that ultimately married his faith with politics. A farmer's son from Carnduff, Saskatchewan, he underwent a conversion at age seventeen when he heard the Calgary school principal and radio evangelist William "Bible Bill" Aberhart preaching on the syndicated *Back to the Bible Hour* radio program. Manning went to Calgary, moved in with Aberhart and his wife, and became one of the first students at Aberhart's Bible college, the Prophetic Bible Institute. Upon graduation he became the preacher's right-hand man, running the school and sometimes handling the radio broadcasts. On air he mimicked Aberhart's delivery so effectively that he became known as "The Echo."

A tall, quietly spoken man whose only hint of secular flamboyance was a liking for gaiters, Manning didn't smoke, drink, or talk publicly about his private life. When he entered provincial politics, he told reporters he didn't have time to think about marriage. Shortly afterward, he married Muriel Aileen Preston, the organist at the Bible Institute.

Politics became a part of Manning's life when Aberhart decided that he should enter politics on a platform of bringing economic relief to depression-battered Albertans through the reform gospel of social credit. With the aid of Manning's considerable organizational skills, and a ready-made constituency base in the churches,

Aberhart's new Social Credit party won fifty-six of sixty-three seats in the province's election of August 1935. Manning became provincial secretary, and at age twenty-six, the youngest cabinet member in the British Empire. Although hampered by a bout of tuberculosis, he acted as the main parliamentary spokesman for the government's program because Aberhart—who detested the combative atmosphere of the legislature preferred to speak in caucus rather than on the floor of the Assembly.

When almost all of the measures introduced by the government to reform the financial system ended in failure, Aberhart became increasingly paranoid and autocratic. Manning found himself acting as the voice of reason, playing advocate for moderates outside the party. Upon Aberhart's death in 1943, Manning, at age thirty-four, became premier. The religious element in Alberta politics was as strong as ever. Manning's first cabinet included a Church of Latter-Day Saints bishop and the Speaker of the legislature was a United Church minister.

Manning quickly took advantage of wartime prosperity to win another election victory by fighting off the left-wing challenge of the populist Co-operative Commonwealth Federation and vigorously opposing the growth of socialism in the West. He then embarked on one last attempt at economic change. The Alberta Bill of Rights Act would have guaranteed Albertans a six-hundred-dollar annual pension, and provided for the licensing and controlling of banks, but the British Privy Council eventually struck it down. Manning quietly put behind him the utopian ideas and unattainable goals that had brought Social Credit to power, and settled down to the task of delivering sound and efficient government. He wasn't a burning enthusiast for parliamentary traditions—he once dismissed the official Opposition as "just a hindrance"—but he revealed himself to be an extraordinarily competent province builder.

The discovery of a major oilfield at Leduc in 1947 finally allowed Alberta to become less reliant on the Eastern banks that purported to dictate Alberta government policy in exchange for keeping the province fiscally afloat. Manning used the resource windfall to improve social services, cultural institutions, and infrastructure. He juggled the demands of the commercial oil interests and the rights of the people of Alberta, skillfully satisfying the interests of both. In 1949 he wrote off $113 million of the province's debt and initiated a program for building roads, schools, and libraries.

During the 1950s, the Manning government continued to pursue a policy of transforming Alberta from a have-not province into an economic powerhouse. This was not good enough for the province's Liberals, led by J. Harper Prowse. Not even the absence of a provincial sales tax nor the short-lived payment of twenty dollars a year from the province's new oil wealth to every adult Albertan could persuade Prowse that Manning's government really had the interests of the province's taxpayers at heart.

In 1955, Prowse levelled a series of wrongdoing and bad management charges against the government. Some of the mud stuck. In the ensuing provincial election, Manning lost fifteen seats to the Liberals—the only time in seven elections as leader that he didn't win by a landslide. However, when a royal commission subsequently cleared the Socred government of almost all wrongdoing, Manning was vindicated. He trounced the Liberals in the 1959 election, and in the process, established himself as a leader of even greater strength than Aberhart.

Though he served as premier for twenty-five years, Manning was always ambivalent about the job because he considered his first calling to be his radio ministry. "The route into politics had been a diversion," wrote his biographer, Lloyd Mackey. "Manning always held the view that both God and the people had some say in how long he would be premier—and he was not about to argue with either." Nor did he argue with the people when they called for something that ran counter to his personal belief system. When the public wanted it, the teetotaler legalized cocktail bars.

Manning stepped down as premier in 1969. He was still at the height of his power in Alberta, though frustrated that his brand of social conservatism had not spread beyond the province's borders to unite the Canadian right. He anointed no successor and with their new leader, Harry Strom, the Socreds were defeated in the ensuing 1971 election when Peter Lougheed's Conservatives rose to power. Manning continued with his radio evangelism and set up a series of government-related agencies with his son, Preston, who was to emerge on the public stage two decades later as the leader of the western-based federal Reform Party.

Manning was appointed in 1970 to the Senate, where he was considered a dour loner though he proved to be a perceptive critic of ambiguities that came before the banking, trade, and commerce committee. When he left the Senate in 1983, having reached the mandatory retirement age of seventy-five, he revealed an unexpected streak of dry Prairie wit, telling reporters, "A lot of people think senators are entirely preoccupied with protocol, alcohol and Geritol." At home, some old Social Crediters claimed to be scandalized when Manning accepted a seat on the board of the Canadian Imperial Bank of Commerce. They said that he could now qualify as one of the "Fifty Big Shots"—the men controlling and manipulating the wealth of Canada who had played an important part in Aberhart's eastern demonology.

In his retirement speech to fellow Socreds, Manning said, "Over the years I have been portrayed by newsmen and commentators as an enigma—reserved, dour, cold and void of emotions. I am happy to report to you that none of these afflictions have ever caused me any pain." He died in February 1996 at age eighty-seven. Preston Manning said in his eulogy that, if his father could offer one last piece of political advice to fellow citizens, it would be this: "Do not let internal discord do to Canada what wars and depressions were unable to do. Continue to build. Continue to build."

Christine Meikle

Developmental education pioneer

1908–1997

A Calgary mother's determination to provide the best possible help for her son with Down syndrome led to a national movement that has spelled support for thousands of Canadians with developmental disabilities.

It began in 1946 when Christine Meikle's son, Roddy, was born with Down syndrome, a chromosomal disorder that often leads to learning difficulties, heart abnormalities, and other problems. Doctors told her that a child with his condition would be better off in an institution, but that was not an option as far as Meikle was concerned. She was a qualified nurse and would care for him herself.

She had trained as a nurse at Montreal's Royal Victoria Hospital after immigrating to Canada at age nineteen from her native Glasgow. She then moved to Calgary where she met and married Bill Meikle, a workplace safety inspector. Christine worked as a nurse at Calgary's Holy Cross Hospital until her children were born. Roddy and his twin sister, Audrey, were the youngest of eight.

Providing an education for Roddy became Meikle's next challenge after the boy turned six. No public school in Calgary would accept him so she decided to start her own. She wasn't a teacher, but she was determined to see her child educated.

She advertised for others who might help. The newspaper ad cost her twenty-four dollars, which she could ill afford, but it paid off when forty people responded. Six were the mothers of children with learning disabilities. One was Emily Follensbee, a teacher and the mother of a six-year-old son with Down syndrome. Follensbee became Meikle's partner in what came to be known as the Kitchen School, located in Meikle's home. There were no desks, just a large oval table and eight kitchen chairs.

Meikle started the school in 1952 without funds, school supplies, or experience. Afterwards, she was quoted as saying that she did have nerve. "I was so pushy. I wrote to oil men asking for donations by return mail." The strategy worked. "We received money from every-one—every men's association." One donor, a man who owned a neighbourhood grocery, supplied cookies, lemonade, and pencils. Other school supplies were handcrafted. Off-duty policemen brought children to and from the Kitchen School. Teachers volunteered their services.

After a year in the Meikle kitchen, the school moved through a succession of church basements and borrowed houses until, in 1958, the eight-classroom Calgary School for Retarded Children opened in northeast Calgary. It was Canada's first government-funded school for the developmentally disabled. Meikle was the first principal. She enrolled in part-time social work and psychology courses at the University of Calgary to learn more about the children placed in her care. "Off and on, I took courses for twenty years," she said. "None of us knew anything about teaching these children. We had no idea of their potential and, at first, we simply used our own common sense as family people."

The school offered the fundamentals of a standard curriculum to Grade Two level, along with training in such basic life skills as dress-ing without help, crossing the street safely, and using public wash-rooms. "We told them stories, taught them social interaction and good manners," said Emily Follensbee. As well as running the school, Meikle also served as founding president of what is now the Developmental Disabilities Resource Centre of Calgary. She laid the groundwork for the provincial and national associations for the neurologically disabled, helped found both the Alberta Association for Community Living and the Vocational and Rehabilitation Research Institute of Calgary, and guided much of the planning for special education across Canada.

In 1961, the school was renamed Christine Meikle School. At that point, it had a student population of 135 served by twelve class-room teachers, three occupational therapists, a part-time speech ther-apist, a caretaker, and six bus drivers. "These children need special facilities and training if they are to become contributing members of society," said Meikle.

A companion school, the Emily Follensbee School, opened in

1964 for children living in the south part of Calgary. Meikle supervised both schools. In 1969, the Calgary Public School Board annexed the two schools. In the years following, Meikle continued to be involved, serving as liaison between the school board and the parents' association.

Meikle received many awards for her work on behalf of the developmentally disabled, including the Order of Canada, an honorary doctorate from the University of Calgary, an Alberta Achievement Award for outstanding service in special education, and the Developmental Disabilities Resource Centre's lifetime distinction award, which Meikle shared with her friend and colleague Emily Follensbee. "I feel kind of guilty accepting honours because so many others helped me," said Meikle. "If I hadn't done it, somebody else would have come along."

Meikle had the satisfaction of seeing her son, Roddy, grow to manhood and become relatively independent, with his own income from a restaurant cleaning job. Follensbee's son, Alan, also achieved a measure of independence, working as a janitor at a community centre.

Meikle's husband, Bill, died in 1979. Four years later she married Tony Harris, a neighbour who had lived next door for fifty years. He died in 1987. Meikle suffered a series of heart attacks in her eighties and died in 1997 at age eighty-eight. Son Roddy, the inspiration for her lifelong devotion to special-needs education, died in December 2000 at age fifty-four.

Pearl Borgal

Athlete, broadcaster, and community volunteer

1910–1993

Because of their pioneering heritage, Albertans are often character-ized as a self-sufficient group of people who can do just about any-thing to which they turn their minds. A notable example is Pearl Borgal, who excelled and broke new ground in many areas of sport-ing and community endeavour—including a radio career in the 1950s when she became Canada's first female sportscaster.

Born Pearl Edmanson in Swift Current, Saskatchewan, she moved to Calgary with her parents when she was a teenager and soon revealed herself to be a remarkably versatile and successful athlete. She won provincial championships in swimming, speed skating, golf, and basketball. She was a member of the Hollies, a female hockey team, in 1926–27 when they won the Western Canadian Championship in Banff. Plus, she ran her own physical-culture school and gymnasium in Calgary. "Nothing is impossible if you set your mind to it," she said. For those who were unable to match her level of achievement, she had another message: "Smile and do your best."

In 1936, at age twenty-six, Borgal moved to Lethbridge as a new bride with her husband, a schoolteacher. She became active in com-munity affairs as a member of the Home and School Association and the Lethbridge Community Council, serving on various civic com-mittees including the town planning commission. "A lot of good can be achieved through volunteering and political action," she said.

During the Second World War, she served as an officer in the Canadian Auxiliary Territorial Service and was president of the Officers' Wives Club in Lethbridge. "A girl can have both a career and a home, if she knows how to put both of them first," she said.

In 1948, Borgal founded the Lethbridge Figure Skating Club and ran it for three years. During the same period, she handled pub-licity for the Lethbridge Exhibition. She organized the first Young

Women's Christian Association chapter in Lethbridge and also the first Victorian Order of Nurses chapter.

Her marriage dissolved in 1952. She returned to Calgary, accompanied by her fourteen-year-old daughter Everal, and joined CKXL Radio as publicity director. From there she soon moved to an on-air job, pioneering in the field of women's sports broadcasting. Her *Women In the World of Sports* commentaries were popular with listeners throughout southern Alberta, as were her sports editorials heard three times daily. She became president of the Calgary branch of the Canadian Women's Press Club and organized the first awards dinners for sports women in Calgary. In 1955, for Alberta's fiftieth anniversary, she organized and served as parade marshal for an all-women's parade.

During the 1960s, Borgal was frequently in the news, promoting amateur sports and organizing the first all-women professional rodeo contests. She served as president of the Canadian Barrel Racing Association and the Canadian Girls' Rodeo Association, and was founding president of the International All-Girls Rodeo League. She was also active in other kinds of community organizations, such as Miles for Millions and Oxfam. She worked on famine relief programs for Biafra and Pakistan, and did volunteer work with Aboriginal peoples. The Sarcees—now known as the Tsuu T'ina Nation—named her Princess Morning Star for her community work on their reserve on the outskirts of Calgary, and they presented her with a ceremonial headdress.

Though she opened many doors for women, Borgal never considered herself a feminist, and disassociated herself from what was then referred to as the women's liberation movement. "I hate the word 'lib,'" she said. "I have always dealt with people and my respect for anyone is as a person, not a man or a woman."

Borgal retired in the mid-1970s, and moved back to Lethbridge. She continued to involve herself in various community activities and organizations, including the Lethbridge Trail Riders, the Ladies' Organization for Civic Improvement, the interestingly named Bombing and Gunnery Riding Club of Lethbridge, and the Lethbridge First organization, which promotes projects to "help keep Lethbridge number one." Perhaps her favourite was the Lethbridge

Keep-in-Touch Society, a telephone network system that she established in 1983 to make daily contact with older people who live alone. In 1986–87, she spearheaded the group that brought the Calgary Wranglers to Lethbridge, renamed them the Hurricanes, and put junior hockey back in the Lethbridge Sportsplex.

As she got older, Borgal became a strong supporter of activities for seniors. The City of Lethbridge presented her with a scroll for "generous and unselfish service to the community" and Lethbridge Community College inducted her into its hall of fame.

In 1991, at age eighty, Borgal was stricken with a degenerative neurological condition that made it impossible for her to carry on with her volunteer activities. She had made her contribution, however, with a long history of community service going back almost sixty years. She died in 1993 at age eighty-two.

Bob Simpson

Radio evangelist

1910–1998

Bob Simpson was the last of the old-time radio evangelists who dominated the airwaves and the political landscape in Alberta between the 1920s and the 1970s. Simpson could lay claim to reaching one of the largest congregations in western North America via a network of Prairie radio stations. He used to tell his fellow ministers, "You fellows have big churches but I've got the biggest one of all."

Simpson's first church, in which he served as a missionary during the 1930s, was in equatorial Africa. Born in Toronto in 1910, he went abroad after graduating from Toronto's Bible College and New York's National Bible Institute. Returning to Canada in 1940, he married his second wife, Marion—his first wife died while they were in Africa—and preached the gospel on Toronto's CHUM radio station before moving west to Lacombe in 1942.

In 1946, Simpson moved to Killam where he ministered at the local Baptist Church. A year later, he accepted an invitation to move to Calgary and take over the *Sunrise Gospel Hour*. The program, broadcast on CFCN Radio, had been started in 1939 by the American evangelist Oscar Lowry who made a big impression in Alberta. During the 1980s, Simpson was still meeting people who became converts of Lowry during the war years.

The *Sunrise* program ran every morning on CFCN, and Simpson filled his allotted time slot with a mixture of live music, Bible instruction, and preaching. A staunch fundamentalist, he spoke out against divorce laws, Sunday movies, and "the philosophy of eat, drink and be merry."

Simpson did most of the radio preaching himself and occasionally brought in big-name evangelists from the United States for guest appearances. These would usually be scheduled in conjunction with giant family rallies in downtown movie theatres. "I can't remember anything else that was so powerful, so full of meaning," said Simpson. "These evangelists had a tremendous influence upon people."

Letters from listeners came from as far away as Alaska. One referred to the program as "Porridge and Sunrise" because of its Pavlovian association with breakfast. "Religion became as important as eating to him," said Simpson.

As well as running the radio ministry, Simpson operated a downtown Christian bookstore, the Sunrise Gospel Bookroom, and was pastor of an inner city, inter-denominational church, Faith Chapel. None of these activities brought him very much money so he went into politics to "put meat and potatoes on the plate."

He chose the Social Credit party because of its long-time association with fellow evangelists Aberhart and Manning. Simpson tried running first for the Socreds at the federal level. When that bid failed, he switched to provincial politics and won a Calgary seat for the Socreds in 1963.

Simpson served in Edmonton for eight years. He lost his seat during the Conservative sweep of Peter Lougheed in 1971, then switched to municipal politics and served as a Calgary alderman for nine years. He lost his northeast ward in 1980 to community worker Bob Hawkesworth, then a twenty-nine-year-old political newcomer, who campaigned successfully against council's "arrogant, insensitive decision to build a forest of high-rises" on land set aside for park development.

After that it was back to full-time pastoring and radio evangelism for Simpson. During the early 1980s he still had a powerful pulpit at CFCN Radio, although the days of daily religious programming were long past. Every Sunday morning, Simpson rose before dawn and preached to a radio congregation estimated at approximately five thousand listeners, down from the ten thousand who tuned in when radio evangelism was in its heyday.

Simpson paid for his radio time on CFCN and also paid for his weekly hour-long broadcasts on stations in Drumheller, High River, Stettler, two stations in Saskatchewan, and one in Manitoba. He depended on donations from listeners to pay for the airtime, and continued to struggle financially as he tried to keep both the radio ministry and the Sunrise Gospel Bookroom operating. "It's basically a library and reading room to complement my radio program," he said. "Some months, I am lucky if it pays the rent and light bill." His reward from the ministry, he said, was the estimated one million dollars that the *Sunrise Gospel Hour* raised during more than four decades on the air. "I've never wanted to build an empire like some of the evangelists, particularly some of them on television, where the real money is."

Simpson lost his CFCN spot in 1984 when the radio station revamped its programming. He was angry about that. "Radio stations have a responsibility and an obligation to make religious shows available," he said. "They say that religious shows interfere with their regular listener patterns but I don't hold to that." He continued to broadcast from other Alberta locations, recording the programs in a friend's basement and shipping them out by mail.

When he turned seventy-eight, Simpson closed the Sunrise Gospel Bookroom. "As you get on, you want to slow down a bit," he said. He also gave up the pastorship of the Faith Chapel, but continued to broadcast his radio program for another year or so until his health failed. He signed off the air in 1989 and retired to Nanaimo, British Columbia, where he died in 1998 at age eighty-eight. By then radio evangelism had virtually disappeared from the airwaves across the Prairies and had given way to television evangelism.

Lillian Knupp

Social historian

1911–1999

Long-living social historians have a great advantage over younger chroniclers in that their memories serve to give a sense of immediacy and vitality to their subjects. Such was the case with James H. Gray, who saw the 1919 Winnipeg General Strike through the eyes of a poverty-stricken youngster who stood in line for food vouchers. It was also true of Grant MacEwan, who lived to be almost ninety-eight and who seemed to have a personal connection with every sod-busting pioneer he ever wrote about. It was certainly true of Lillian Knupp, the scribe of High River, whose roots in Medicine Tree Country (as that part of southern Alberta is commonly known) ran deep and strong.

Lillian's paternal grandfather, J. W. Short, was the first white settler to homestead on the south side of the Highwood River. He came from Selkirk, Manitoba, in 1883, and combined farming with serving as the area's first justice of the peace. He also served on the boards of the first school and church. Her father, Charles Short, was recruited at age fifteen to serve in the Alberta militia that battled Aboriginal peoples and Métis in the 1885 Northwest Rebellion. He later served as mayor and councillor of the new town of High River.

Lillian won a writing prize at age eight, when she entered a contest sponsored by a farm journal, and that seemed to sow the seeds for what she would do later in life. She edited the school yearbook while attending High River High School, and continued to do some writing and editing while taking courses in political economy and history at Mount Royal College in Calgary. She met Nellie McClung during this period, and never forgot the advice the famous author and suffragist gave her about writing: "She told me that a writer should never be without a certain something. Then she lifted up her skirts to show that she had a pencil and notebook tucked into her garter!"

In 1932, Lillian married Charles Burchill, a history professor at Mount Royal College. They moved to Brooks, adopted two infant boys, and collaborated on articles for newspapers, magazines, and university quarterlies across Canada. In 1940, Charles became a flight instructor with the Royal Canadian Air Force, which led to postings across Canada for the duration of the Second World War. During this period, Lillian and Charles separated and divorced.

In 1945, Lillian came back to High River as a single mother with her two sons. She worked at a restaurant for a while and then took a job at the weekly *High River Times*, though not initially as a writer or editor. The paper needed a bookkeeper and Lillian did that job until she left in 1957 to work as a staff sergeant with a militia training unit. "They offered a typing course, and I felt it would help me brush up." In the meantime, she married Alex Knupp, a High River farmer and freight transport business owner, and they added three foster sons to their family. She often said that her work was "almost a hobby" and that her prime concern was for giving children a good start in life. One of her foster sons, Allan Kaye, is Cree and he recalled that his mother always made a point of having special teaching available for him, so that he would know about his Native heritage. "She taught me about my culture," he said.

She returned to the *Times* in 1965, as news editor, and over the next three decades she maintained an association with the paper either as an employee or as a freelance contributor. During the same period she began contributing to local community history projects as a research historian, writer, and editor.

In 1984, when Lillian was seventy-three, she introduced some of her work as a historian to readers of the *Times* by launching a weekly column of social history and comment that she titled "Medicine Tree Country." She took the name from the traditional symbol of High River: a freak of nature in which two old cottonwood trees are joined as one by a connecting branch. This medicine tree stood in a glade west of High River and was worshipped by Natives for more than a century as a healing shrine. It was partially salvaged in rotting old age for preservation in what is now George Lane Memorial Park.

In her column, Knupp introduced readers to hundreds of colourful characters from High River's past, and occasionally unlocked the closet housing the community's skeletons. In one column, for example, she wrote about a member of her own family, a certain Uncle Willy, who accidentally burned down High River's only school. When some readers suggested she should exercise more discretion in terms of what should be revealed and what should remain under wraps, she retorted, "These people had weaknesses as well as virtues. Neither should be glossed over."

She also bristled at suggestions that because her columns dwelt in the past, they only appealed to seniors. "Judging by my not inconsiderable correspondence from Alberta schoolchildren, I think that for the present time I'll stick to the style of writing which has attracted their response."

As well as being the town's historian, social conscience, and resident expert on local landmarks, Knupp was an energetic community volunteer, active in such organizations as the High River Legion, the Pioneers and Oldtimers Association, the Agricultural Society, and the Chamber of Commerce. She was president of the Alberta Progressive Conservative Women's Association during the 1970s and recalled proudly that the future premier, Peter Lougheed, launched his successful 1971 campaign during a conference call that she organized for him in the publisher's office of the *High River Times*.

She was also a business proprietor. When her husband Alex died in 1972, she took over the running of the farm and the freight transport business. At the same time, she ran the Canadian Pacific Railway's High River freight office.

She continued to write her newspaper column even when her failed eyesight made it impossible for her to read her research notes, and her deteriorating hearing made it difficult for her to hear the bell on her typewriter that warned of an approaching right-hand margin. "I manage with the aid of a very obliging proof-reader," she said.

She wrote her last column just a few days before her death in January 1999 at age eighty-seven. She was in the High River Hospital at the time, and with characteristic determination, she left her hospital bed to get the column to the paper before deadline. The column gave no hint that she knew she was near the end. It dealt with lobbying governments and with citizens speaking up for their civil rights. It did include a tribute to her father who "had given a great deal to his community, both privately and in public service." From him she had learned that she should do the same.

Compilations of Knupp's columns for the *High River Times* have been published in book form under such titles as *Roots of the Medicine Tree* and *Twigs of the Medicine Tree*.

Max Bell

Businessman and philanthropist

1912–1972

During the 1960s, Max Bell had the highest profile of any business-man in Calgary. He owned a major portion of Canada's biggest news-paper chain, a string of successful racehorses, and a large block of shares in the Canadian Pacific Railway (CPR). Yet few Calgarians could have picked him out in a crowd. He hated having his picture taken, and rarely granted newspaper interviews. Like many million-aires who have lived in Calgary, Bell liked to walk around in public without being recognized.

He was a self-made millionaire. His once-wealthy father had owned a chain of dailies in the West, but at the time of his death in 1935, his last remaining paper, the *Calgary Albertan,* was five hun-dred thousand dollars in debt.

Max earned a commerce degree at McGill University in 1932, and then moved to British Columbia, where he worked as a labourer and prospector. He also played hockey with the Kimberley Dynamiters of the Western International League for two years, and impressed the sportswriters with his prowess on the football field. "He kicked the ball so far and high that, on late autumn afternoons, it came down covered with snowflakes," wrote the columnist Jim Coleman.

Bell moved to Calgary, just before his father's death, to become business manager of the ailing *Albertan.* Eight years later, with the help of four friends, he raised enough money to buy the paper. By 1945, he had repaid all his father's debts.

In 1947, Imperial Oil discovered oil in Leduc, and Bell's invest-ments in this black gold yielded a fortune. He used the profits to make the *Albertan* the nucleus of his own newspaper chain. In 1950, he purchased the two newspapers in Victoria, British Columbia, the morning *Colonist* and the afternoon *Daily Times.* Nine years later, he pooled his newspaper holdings with those of Victor Sifton and

Richard Malone of the *Winnipeg Free Press* to form FP Publications. By the mid-1960s, more Canadians read FP newspapers than any other. The chain, which included the *Ottawa Journal, Vancouver Sun, Lethbridge Herald,* and the *Globe and Mail,* was sold to the Thomson Corporation in 1980.

Although he claimed that his business life was full of "hare-brained mistakes," Bell rarely faltered. His only known failure in the newspaper business occurred during the 1940s when he borrowed money to acquire the failing *Edmonton Bulletin.* He shut down the paper after four money-losing years, denouncing the printers' wage demands as too exorbitant for a marginal operation.

Bell also admitted to a youthful business mistake made during his prospecting days in British Columbia, when a confidence man swindled him out of six ounces of gold, but such mistakes were the exception. He was one of the original developers and owners of Alberta Eastern Natural Gas Company, which drilled successfully for natural gas in southeastern Alberta. He was the largest individual shareholder of the CPR at one point, and came within 2 percent of acquiring the Bay. However, he changed his mind at the last moment because he didn't want to manage the retail giant himself. A self-described "fast-in, fast-out plunger," Bell explained that he was happier making deals than running things.

An interest in thoroughbred horse breeding and racing gave Bell a high profile internationally. He ran a horse farm in Okotoks in partnership with oilman Frank McMahon, and then moved into the big leagues with jockey Johnny Longden, and crooner Bing Crosby. His stable's colours were a familiar sight across North America and abroad. In 1961, a Bell and McMahon horse, Four and Twenty, won the Santa Anita Derby. Other horses from their stable won the Irish Derby, the Coronation Stakes, and in 1968, the Queen's Plate. Bell's other sporting involvements included part ownership of the Vancouver Canucks hockey team, and the creation of Hockey Canada, of which he was the first chairman.

A lifelong fitness buff, Bell often exercised during board meetings. When he turned fifty, he celebrated his birthday by shooting a round of golf, playing five sets of tennis, swimming thirty lengths, running a measured mile in six minutes, and finishing off with a game of touch football. His day's activity ended when he suffered a shoulder separation while trying to catch a pass.

He never smoked or drank. Sports columnist Jim Coleman wrote, "His idea of an orgy of self-indulgence was to sit in his suite at the Palliser, and order up three different flavours of ice cream in the same dish. He'd sit grinning amiably while his friends assuaged their own thirst with sturdier potables."

His private life, which he carefully guarded from prying eyes, centred on two marriages, six children, collecting artworks by Krieghoff and Remington, making home movies, playing with his large model railroad, reading the Bible and the *Daily Racing Form*, and contributing time and money to Grace Presbyterian Church in Calgary. He led the Canada-wide institution of synods, which gave rise to the expansion of the Presbyterian Church in the 1950s and 1960s.

Bell was just fifty-nine when he died in July 1972 of brain disease at the Montreal Neurological Institute. He donated the bulk of his twenty-two-million-dollar estate to the Max Bell Foundation, a charitable organization that he had created in 1965 to support a wide range of projects and institutions. The foundation has donated more than fifty-two million dollars thus far, giving the Max Bell name to a hockey arena, a drama theatre, and an addiction treatment centre in Calgary; a performing arts building at the Banff Centre; an aquatic centre at the University of Lethbridge; a medical research building at the Toronto General Hospital; and a chair of journalism at the University of Regina.

The foundation has been based in Calgary since May 1997, after operating out of Ontario for more than a decade, and it continues to reflect the philosophy of its founder in its mission as a self-styled "venture capitalist of philanthropy."

"The only time money is important is when you haven't any," said Max Bell. "Once you have it, however, you must accept the responsibility to make the best use of it, and to ensure that those who become dependent on you for a livelihood are not injured by your transactions."

Dr. Dave Lander

Country doctor

1912–1993

Alcoholism was rarely seen as a medical problem before Dr. Dave Lander started treating alcoholics in the 1940s. He was one of the first physicians in Canada to recognize and foster the concept of problem drinking as a medical disorder worthy of informed and objective medical care.

Lander was a medical maverick whose specialty was people, a country doctor who knew all about modern diagnosis and treatment and also had a rare understanding of human emotions.

"You can't practise good medicine without looking into the heart too," he said. That's where he would see the emotional strife that often gave rise to physical symptoms. Dr. Dave (that's how he always asked his patients to address him) estimated that frustration, shame, or loneliness caused 30 percent of common ailments. Yet those emotional factors often went unrecognized.

Lander had his own share of emotional strife before he became a physician. Born into a Jewish family in Russia in 1912, he witnessed the organized persecution and harassment of Jews during the First World War. "We came through a lot of tribulation and hardship during that time," he said afterward. "I don't talk about the bloodshed I saw. These unforgettable experiences still haunt my dreams and nightmares."

His family fled Russia via Poland and Belgium in 1924 and settled in Winnipeg where his father, who had been a merchant, worked as a labourer. Young Dave, then aged twelve, didn't speak a word of English and was put in a public school grade four class where he struggled initially. "It was sink or swim."

Eventually he made it through school and with financial help from his cousin, a general practitioner in Black Diamond, Alberta, he took medicine at the University of Manitoba. It was, he said, about the only career option available to him at the time. Anti-Semitism was rife in Canada. Jewish lawyers were excluded from most firms, there were scarcely any Jewish teachers, and Jewish nurses, engineers, and architects had to hide their identity to find jobs in their fields.

Lander completed his medical studies at the University of Alberta in Edmonton, and came close to flunking because he could not kill dogs for medical experimentation as required by the program. "I had to bribe my classmates to put my dogs to sleep," he said. "If my professor had ever discovered that, I'm sure he would have thrown me out. Fortunately, he never did."

After graduation in 1937, Lander got the best job he could find—at a mental institution near Edmonton—so he could help his parents out financially. That job bored him. He saw himself as a jailer, with a big ring of keys in his office and his patients incarcerated like criminals. "This was before the day of tranquilizers and open-door policies. Everyone was under lock and key." He returned to university part-time to earn some pharmaceutical qualifications and then moved to Black Diamond to join the practice of his cousin, Harry.

Dr. Dave enjoyed working in Black Diamond and neighbouring Turner Valley. With the help of two nurses, he helped build up the local community hospital, now the Oilfields General Hospital, and gradually he added the hospital treatment of alcoholics to his work as a general practitioner. The hospital was small, only twenty-three beds, but Dr. Dave managed to arrange it so that alcoholics from all over the province could be treated without denying service to local residents.

His approach to the treatment of alcoholics was marvellously simple. He did it, he said, "by listening." Every doctor should have the "three Hs—humanity, humility, and humour," and should also be a good listener. He used the same approach in his treatment, years later, of the effects of psychosomatic illnesses and geriatric complaints.

Dr. Dave's reputation spread far beyond the ranches and oil fields of Black Diamond and Turner Valley. His pioneering work in the treatment of alcoholics resulted in his name being given to an alcohol treatment centre in Claresholm. He was written up in newspaper articles, profiled in a radio documentary, and recognized by *Reader's*

Digest magazine as one of its famous unforgettable characters. "The best possible kind of doctor for today's troubled world," said the magazine, noting his sense of obligation to the community in which he lived, and his humanitarian concern for all patients "whether they be respected judge, condemned criminal, or alcoholic." In 1991, he received the Order of Canada for embodying a "compassionate, humanitarian approach toward the treatment of illness."

A self-styled "caring maverick—a young colt who kicks up his heels," Dr. Dave occasionally courted controversy by criticizing his peers for the way they treated the elderly. He was especially critical of doctors who prescribed excessive medication as a cure for certain geriatric conditions. "We look upon old people as bags of bones," he said. "Better understanding is needed."

Dr. Dave never married. "He gave us his whole life," said a former patient. Nor did he willingly retire. When he left the practice in Black Diamond at age fifty-eight, primarily because he had a bad heart, Dr. Dave moved to Calgary, rented rooms in the Palliser Hotel, and carried on with some of the work he had been doing before. He counselled alcoholics, saw the occasional patient ("human rejects that nobody else wants to touch"), and gave lectures on alcoholism, psychosomatic problems, and the problems of the aged.

He wrote about his own aging in an article for *Reader's Digest* about the joys of riding free on the buses, getting discount tickets to the movies, and getting free passes to the zoo. "I lost neither my health nor my wits on my sixty-fifth birthday," he wrote. "Presidents and prime ministers have served with distinction in their seventies. Judges have rendered important decisions in their eighties. Although I have retired from general practice, I too have something to offer because my medical knowledge remains much in demand."

When he turned seventy-one, Dr. Dave received a twenty-five-thousand-dollar award from the Alberta Heritage Savings Trust Fund "for your lifetime commitment to healing the sick and assisting the helpless." He knew immediately what he would do with the money: "It will allow me to be a freelance ambassador of goodwill who pleads for a better understanding of the alienated, the depressed, the alcoholics, and the rejected."

He completed a memoir before his heart and a degenerative joint disease forced him to ease up. It never found a publisher. If it did, he wanted the title to be *My Specialty is People: Memoirs of a Medical Maverick*. Dr. Dave died in July 1993 at age eighty-one. The Turner Valley swimming pool bears his name.

William Hawrelak

Businessman and mayor

1915–1975

William Hawrelak was the "Comeback Kid" of Edmonton municipal politics, twice forced to quit the mayor's office because of questionable land dealings yet still able to rebound because he refused to
admit defeat and the voters were ready to ignore past misdeeds.
Rarely has an Alberta politician had a career so dappled with highs
and lows, triumphs and scandals.

In 1951, Hawrelak won his first mayoralty election. He polled
the largest number of votes ever cast up to that point for an
Edmonton mayoralty candidate. He was also the first mayor of
Ukrainian descent to be elected in Western Canada. "In some parts
of Canada, his name would have been against him," observed an
editorial writer for a Calgary newspaper. "But in fast-growing, for-
ward-looking and progressive Edmonton all that mattered was his
ability."

His ability to succeed against all odds was a defining characteristic of Hawrelak's life. Born in a farming community about 120
kilometres northeast of Edmonton, he was the son of Ukrainian
immigrants who came to Canada at the turn of the century. He
worked on the family farm as a stopgap measure after he completed
high school because other jobs were hard to find during the Great
Depression. Hawrelak was determined to get off the farm. He kept
writing letters to politicians and government officials until the
Alberta Liquor Control Board finally rewarded his persistence in
1936 by offering him a job behind the counter at a liquor store in
Edmonton.

Hawrelak's career with the liquor board, which took him from
counter work to accounting department duties, ended in 1938 when
his father developed a heart condition and Bill opted to return home
to take charge of the family farm. He remained there until after the
Second World War and became active in local community life as a

co-founder of the Alberta Farmers' Union, as a school trustee, and as a wartime organizer of Victory Bond campaigns.

In 1945, Hawrelak rented the farm to a neighbour and moved to Edmonton with his wife, Pearl, and seven-year-old daughter, Jeanette. He took the money he had saved from farming and with his brother-in-law, Mike Shandro, bought a small soft-drink bottling company, Prairie Rose Manufacturing, which held the Edmonton franchise for Orange Crush. Bill and Pearl bought a bungalow in the King Edward district of Edmonton and at the first meeting of the local community association Bill found himself acclaimed as president.

His lobbying for an extension of city sewer lines and garbage service to Edmonton's new subdivisions took Hawrelak from community politics into the mainstream civic arena. "Get on council," people told him, "and you'll get results."

He was defeated in his first bid for an aldermanic seat but succeeded on his second try, in 1949, at age thirty-four. In the meantime, Hawrelak added to his public service credentials by actively lobbying for a Trans-Canada Highway route through Edmonton and Jasper, and by serving as a director for the Edmonton Federation of Community Leagues.

Hawrelak was a showman at heart, and his strategy as an alderman—in contrast to his reserved colleagues on city council—was to constantly look for what today would be called media "photo opportunities." One of his early publicity stunts was to have Edmonton salute the seventy-fifth anniversary of Fort Calgary with a float in the Calgary Stampede Parade featuring a giant birthday cake topped by the 1950 Miss Edmonton. By keeping a high profile, and filling in for the mayor at every opportunity, Hawrelak positioned himself well for a successful run for the mayoralty office in 1951.

Edmonton was the fastest-growing city in Canada when Hawrelak became mayor. The discovery of oil at nearby Leduc in 1947 had resulted in a period of unprecedented expansion. Acquiring the financing needed for huge capital expenditures on roads, sewers, water lines, and off-street parking became one of Hawrelak's biggest challenges during his first term. In 1952, Edmonton's per capita debt was the highest in the country. "A situation without parallel in the history of municipal government in Canada," said a city commissioner.

Hawrelak was re-elected by acclamation in 1953 and again in 1955. During that time the city spent millions of dollars on new roads, bridges, sidewalks, storm sewers, sewage and water treatment facilities, improvements to the city-owned Royal Alexandra Hospital, a new football stadium, baseball grandstands, and a new city hall. The *Edmonton Journal* editorialized that with more rapid growth still to come, the city should "count itself fortunate" to have Hawrelak at the helm.

In June 1957, Hawrelak tried to repeat his municipal success at the federal level by running for the Liberals in a federal election, but he narrowly lost to Ambrose Holowach of Social Credit. Later that year, Hawrelak won a fourth term as mayor. During that term his close involvement with various land dealings—both as a land owner himself, and as a civic official with the power to influence rezoning applications—caused him to become the subject of a judicial inquiry. Hawrelak had invested extensively in commercial properties that he either resold at a profit or used for hotel and apartment building. Caught in the explosion of Edmonton's business growth, Hawrelak seemed unaware that it was hardly appropriate for the mayor to be operating as a land developer.

The judicial inquiry occurred after an Edmonton motel owner, Ed Leger, discovered that Hawrelak's brother-in-law had acquired a parcel of city-owned property that was then rezoned for motel use. Leger spent the next year looking through city hall records for other land transactions that might be questionable, and uncovered several suspicious cases. The matter was then turned over to a judge, Marshall M. Porter, who ruled in 1959 that Hawrelak was guilty of "gross misconduct" when he used his influence to have a parcel of city property transferred to his brother-in-law for motel construction. Porter also ruled that Hawrelak acted improperly in five other land deals. Hawrelak responded by tendering his resignation as mayor while publicly proclaiming his innocence. City council sued for $133,000—his estimated profit on three of the deals. Hawrelak settled out of court for one hundred thousand dollars.

Hawrelak spent the next four years in political limbo before deciding the time was ripe to make a comeback. Admitting that some of his land dealings had been "politically unwise" and promising "there will not be a repetition of this in the future," he ran for his fifth term as mayor in 1963 and handily defeated an alderman named Stan Milner. The following year, Hawrelak defeated a former federal cabinet minister to win his sixth term as mayor.

Because Hawrelak continued his land dealings both before and after he returned to the mayor's office, it seemed inevitable that it would be only a matter of time before he was in trouble again. However, this time it was a technical breach of the City Act—not so much his own misdeeds—that brought him down. Because he owned more than a 25 percent interest in a company that sold land to the city for park use, he violated a section of the City Act that was later repealed. That minor offence was enough to have him disqualified from holding public office, and his opponents on city council saw to it that he was duly removed. In 1965, for the second time in his political career, Hawrelak left the mayor's chair under a cloud.

Hawrelak made his next comeback bid in 1966, but now he faced an additional challenge because the city was suing him over yet another questionable land deal, this time involving his participation in a land exchange for a new city subdivision. The Supreme Court of Canada would rule later that Hawrelak was guilty of no wrongdoing because the land exchange took place while he was out of office. However, that didn't help him in 1966. He lost the election to Vince Dantzer, a former alderman who had assumed the mayor's chair when Hawrelak was disqualified.

With that loss, it seemed that Hawrelak's political career was finally over, but he still had one more card to play. In 1974, after eight years in the political wilderness, he announced his intention to run again for the position he had held for six terms. An Edmonton newsmagazine commented, "Edmonton has not had another mayor who has left so profound a mark on the face of the city, nor one so deeply touched by scandal." The old magic was still there. Hawrelak won the mayoralty race in a landslide, capturing 49 percent of the popular vote. At age fifty-nine he was on top again.

The Supreme Court finally exonerated him in March 1975, ten years after the city sued him for conflict of interest, but the victory celebration was short-lived. High blood pressure and the grueling pace he set for himself as mayor began to take their toll. In November

1975, Hawrelak suffered a heart attack and died. "He had made mistakes and suffered great personal anguish," reported the *Edmonton Report*. "Yet in every sense he had died in the city's service as a result. And, in the hearts of its citizens, the record stood clear. The blemishes were gone."

Bruno Engler

Mountain guide and photographer

1915–2001

Bruno Engler was the last of Canada's legendary Swiss mountain guides, the pipe-smoking alpine experts who first started coming to this country in the late 1890s to work for the Canadian Pacific Railway (CPR), leading tourists up the previously unscaled peaks of the Rocky Mountains. He was also a skilled photographer and an engaging storyteller, and it is for these accomplishments too that Engler will be remembered as having played a significant role in the cultural history of Canada's western mountains.

The Swiss guides had been a part of Rocky Mountain life for forty years when Engler emigrated from Switzerland in 1939. They acquired their mountaineering skills in the Alps and were hired by the CPR to provide professional assistance to inexperienced climbers who wanted to try mountaineering in one of the most stunning alpine settings in the world.

Engler, a studio photographer's son from Lugano, became interested in mountains as a child, accompanying his father on expeditions to photograph Swiss alpine scenery. He hiked and climbed at every opportunity, and learned to ski while in his teens. Like his father, he then became a photographer, but because he disliked the solitude of the darkroom, decided to broaden his career options by becoming a mountain guide and ski instructor. Mountain climbing had become popular in Europe after an English engraver named Edward Whymper made the first ascent of the Matterhorn in 1865.

A friend named Molly Nolet encouraged Engler to move to Canada. She had seen CPR advertising brochures claiming that Banff was the St. Moritz of Canada, and she undertook to visit the area and find out more. She wrote back in the spring of 1939 to say that Banff had lots of opportunities for a mountain guide and ski instructor with Engler's skills. With war clouds gathering over Europe, Engler didn't take much persuading. He set sail for Canada on the Empress of Britain, and set up house with Molly near Invermere. He spent the summer working as a guide for the Brewster Transport Company at the Columbia Icefield, and spent the winter guiding and teaching skiing west of Banff at Sunshine Village, then a small ski operation.

Engler became an assistant guide at Lake Louise in the summer of 1940, returned to Sunshine in the winter, and quickly became known as a top ski instructor and a beer-drinking *bon vivant*. Molly didn't take to the mountain way of life in quite the same way. She made regular trips to Vancouver to get away from the cold and the isolation, and eventually she stopped coming back.

Tourism in the Rockies ground to a standstill during the Second World War. Engler moved east to teach skiing in the Quebec Laurentians. In 1944, he enlisted in the Canadian army and was sent back to the Rockies to teach mountain warfare and survival to troops bound for Europe. After his discharge in 1946, Engler returned to guiding at Lake Louise and skiing at Sunshine. Tourism had picked up again and some of the best climbers in the world began to arrive in the Rockies looking for guides. They included the British Everest climber, Frank Smythe; American K2 climber, Tony Cromwell; and his partner, Georgia Englehard, who had excelled as a climber in Europe.

In 1949, Engler married Angel Clarke, a Banff bank clerk. They settled initially in the Crowsnest Pass, where Engler worked as a strip miner and helped develop a ski area. At the same time he rekindled his interest in photography. In 1951, he moved with Angel and their two-year-old daughter to Edmonton, where he took a job as a government photographer taking still photographs of the agriculture industry, and shooting footage for training and advertising films.

Engler broke into movies in 1953 when assigned by the province to help with the production of *Far Country*, a Hollywood western shot in the Athabasca Glacier area of the Columbia Icefield. Engler worked as a location scout and mountain safety consultant, and became hooked on the film business. He quit his government job in 1955, moved with his expanding family—which now included two more children—to the Canmore area, and worked as a cinematographer and cameraman on such films as Disney's *White Wilderness* and the National Film Board documentary *The David Thompson*

Story. Between movies Engler shot still images for local tourism and publishing clients and did portraits of well-known locals.

From the 1960s onward, Engler became well known in the Bow Valley region for his work in films, still photography, skiing, and mountain safety. He also achieved a kind of legendary status as a storyteller, with his endless stream of anecdotes about encounters with grizzlies, movie stars, and assorted men and women of the mountains. He was the subject of numerous newspaper and magazine articles, and the CBC made a half-hour television special about him entitled "Diary of a Mountain Man." His family grew to eight children but long absences and constant financial difficulty strained his relationship with Angel, and in 1973 they divorced.

Engler married North Carolina-born Adrienne Day in the mid-1970s and had two more children. He was sixty-seven when his tenth child was born in 1982. That marriage foundered too, because of money problems and the amount of time Engler spent away from home. In 1985, Adrienne departed for North Carolina with the children, and Engler entered a long period of depression. He had to keep working because he was almost broke, but a worsening heart condition and a nagging knee problem made it increasingly difficult for him to do so.

One reason for his poverty was his generosity. The film business was never steady enough for Engler to make a living from it, so he relied on his still photography to support himself and his family. Then, however, he gave his images away for next to nothing because he couldn't bring himself to charge a lot of money for them. When the Whyte Museum of the Canadian Rockies finally bought a large body of his work, he still wouldn't push his prices up to where they belonged. Friends had to negotiate the price upward whenever they tried to help him out by buying one of his prints.

Engler didn't climb or ski much after age seventy-two because of his heart and knee problems. Still he remained an active member of the mountaineering community, a sought-after tour guide and convention speaker, and a regular patron of ski and mountaineering events in Banff. Every year he would preside over the annual Veterans' Race for "older" skiers at Sunshine Village, an event that he had started in 1966. He received many awards for his contributions to Canadian mountaineering, including the Summit of Excellence Award at the Banff Festival of Mountain Films.

In 1996, when he was eighty-one, Engler married Vera Matrasovà, a film archivist and former Olympian from Czechoslovakia. The same year, the Alpine Club of Canada published *A Mountain Life*, a chronicle of Engler's life in the mountains as recorded in his photographs and stories. "The best part about the book was finishing it," joked Engler. He dedicated it to his children, to his new wife Vera, and to the memory of Angel, the mother of eight of his children.

He died in March 2001 at age eighty-five. Alpine historian Bob Sandford, who edited and added biographical material to Engler's book, said his life was a testament to the grace that can be achieved by long and intimate association with the mountains. "He helped people understand the joy and extraordinary glory of what can happen to you in these remarkable places." Though he rubbed shoulders with such big-name visitors to the mountains as Pierre Trudeau, Marilyn Monroe, Paul Newman, and Jimmy Stewart, Engler's admiration was always reserved for the mountains not the visitors. "Never forget," he said, "that the mountain is still the master. Mountains make people look small—very, very small."

Ruth Carse

Dance teacher and choreographer

1916–1999

When Ruth Carse founded the Alberta Ballet in 1966, she resolved that it should serve the entire province, not just Calgary and Edmonton. She said the same thing when she founded the Alberta Ballet School in 1971. Bringing dance to people throughout her native province became her life's work after Carse's career as a dancer was abruptly terminated by injury when she was in her thirties.

Born into a musical family in Edmonton, Carse sang around the piano as a child with her mother, and took lessons in highland dance at the encouragement of her Scottish-born father who worked as a plumber. At age six she switched to ballet, learning from Madame Boucher who rolled back the carpets and taught classes in her living room. From then on Carse's career direction was set. Though she said in later years that she never really planned to become a professional dancer, Carse was talented enough to perform on the stages of Toronto and New York.

After leaving Madame Boucher, Carse studied ballet in Edmonton with two sisters named Kinney who had trained in Toronto. She danced at the Kinney School throughout her teens and also performed at other venues in Edmonton. At age twenty-one, she was encouraged to continue with her studies, which meant leaving Alberta. Her father bet her a hundred dollars that she would be back home within a month. Carse won the bet. She later said that moving to Toronto was the best thing that ever happened to her.

In Toronto, she studied with Boris Volkoff, a Russian-born dancer and choreographer who operated a ballet school and company. She danced with the company for ten years, performing throughout Ontario, and like the other dancers in the company, never received any pay. All the dancers had day jobs and rehearsed and performed at night and on weekends. Carse worked for a Toronto advertising firm and eventually became a manager there

149

while simultaneously maintaining her position as soloist with one of Canada's first ballet companies. She spent her summer vacations studying dance in London.

In 1949, Carse won a scholarship to the prestigious American School of Ballet in New York. She landed a job with the Yiddish Theatre in Brooklyn, and danced in a new musical every week. She also performed as a member of Radio City Music Hall's ballet corps, and for the first time in her life, she was paid to dance. The pay was low—she subsisted on a diet of cheese and shredded wheat—but the experience was invaluable. Between shows at Radio City, Carse travelled uptown by bus to take ballet classes at Carnegie Hall.

Carse returned to Canada in 1952 to join the newly formed National Ballet of Canada but her career there lasted only three months. She quit to train in Toronto as a ballet teacher with Gweneth Lloyd, founder of the Royal Winnipeg Ballet. Eventually Carse began teaching while continuing to perform as a dancer. She appeared in some of the first variety shows presented on CBC Television.

In the summer of 1954, while Carse was studying in England, she tore her Achilles tendon and that put an end to her performing career. Shortly afterwards she was invited to come back to Edmonton to teach at the dance school of a friend who was on maternity leave. Edmonton remained her home and the centre of Carse's work in dance for the next forty years.

She choreographed Broadway musicals for the Edmonton Light Opera Company and formed a young amateur ensemble called Dance Interlude, which toured throughout Alberta. In 1961, Dance Interlude was renamed the Edmonton Ballet. In 1966, Carse secured support from the Alberta government to fund what would eventually become a fully professional ballet company serving the entire province, and the Edmonton Ballet became the Alberta Ballet. It took another five years, however, before there was money in the company budget to actually pay the dancers. Nevertheless, the Alberta Ballet flourished under Carse's artistic leadership and soon gained recognition as one of Canada's top ballet companies. As choreographer Anne Flynn has noted, "It was a volunteer company that survived on the energy of its participants, its audiences and the undaunted determination of Ms. Carse."

In 1971, Carse founded the Alberta Ballet School. Four years later, she resigned as artistic director of the Alberta Ballet to focus her energies on training young dancers, many of whom later went on to work at dance schools and companies all over the world. At the same time, she continued to choreograph ballets for the company.

Carse was determined that ballet would become accessible to the people of her province, particularly underprivileged children. As well as serving as principal of the Alberta Ballet School, she created dance programs for Edmonton's Alex Taylor School for needy children. She also taught at Victoria Composite High School and the University of Alberta. Additionally, she travelled the world as an examiner for London's Royal Academy of Dance, looking for talented youngsters who would benefit from high-level training.

Carse served as principal of the Alberta Ballet School until 1986 when she turned seventy. She spent the first part of her retirement teaching privately, coaching, adjudicating, and consulting in Edmonton. She then moved to Ponoka to live with her sister. Never married, Ruth had been engaged before the Second World War but her fiancé was killed in the conflict. In 1991, on her seventy-fifth birthday, she received the Order of Canada. "Her determination and vision have made her a pioneer in the dance world," said the citation. She died in November 1999 at age eighty-two.

Neil "Scotty" Munro

Hockey coach

1917–1975

Junior hockey emerged as an amateur league sport in Alberta at the start of the First World War. Communities started the league as a way of ensuring that their ice arenas would not fall empty when players of intermediate and senior calibre were called away to serve in the war. It thrived up to the 1930s, when hockey fans across the province regularly turned out in droves to watch young players who might one day star in the National Hockey League. It continued to flourish in the 1940s, when NHL teams began direct sponsorship of junior clubs and improved the quality of play. Then it went through a period of decline when junior hockey in Alberta seemed to consist of the Detroit Red Wings-sponsored Edmonton Oil Kings and little else. However, that changed for the better during the mid-1960s, with the emergence of the Western Canada Junior Hockey League as a unifying force for junior hockey on the Prairies. Much of the credit for that development goes to a coach and hockey visionary named Neil "Scotty" Munro.

Munro, nicknamed Scotty because his father played the bagpipes professionally, devoted his life to hockey. Anything else that he did—sell encyclopedias, manage a bowling alley, work in an oil refinery—was all in the cause of supporting his involvement in hockey.

Born on a farm near Cabri, Saskatchewan, in 1917, Munro learned his hockey in the community arena of nearby Shackleton where he played as a goaltender. When he was twenty, he moved to Melville, where he married Rose Bashnick, a fellow hockey enthusiast who proved to be his strongest ally when he later became a coach. Whenever Scotty was suspended from the game, which happened frequently over the course of his long coaching career, Rose filled in for him behind the bench.

In 1939, Scotty and Rose moved to Yorkton, Saskatchewan, where he made his coaching debut with a Midget team. The game subsequently took him back and forth through small-town Saskatchewan and Alberta, where exhibition games became his bread and butter. Scratching a living from hockey wasn't easy, but somehow Scotty managed.

He managed because he knew how to sell the game. Munro was a showman and a propagandist. Whenever a reporter phoned up asking for a quote, Munro was always happy to comply. "I've got my job to do, and you guys have got yours," he would say. "Just remember to spell the name of the team right. And mention the next game."

His coaching career took him first from Yorkton to Moose Jaw and then, in 1947, to Lethbridge, where his team, the Native Sons, became the first hockey team in history to charter a plane for a game, a national junior finals game that they played in Vancouver. He left Lethbridge in 1948 and moved to Bellevue in the Crowsnest Pass where he coached the local Lions until they folded in 1950. After that he moved back to Saskatchewan, where he remained for the next eighteen years, coaching first in Humboldt and then in Estevan. He showed his community spirit when he spearheaded construction of a new arena in Estevan. He also showed his volatile temperament, which brought him numerous suspensions—once for hitting a referee.

In 1966, the Western Canada Junior Hockey League (WCJHKL) arose from the remnants of the recently disbanded Saskatchewan Junior Hockey League. The chief organizers were Munro, Winnipeg financier Ben Hatskin, and the general manager of the Edmonton Oil Kings, Bill Hunter. The Canadian Amateur Hockey Association refused to give the new league its official blessing because certain teams from the old SJHL were not included, but this didn't bother Munro and his colleagues. They signed up seven teams in Alberta and Saskatchewan, and ran the WCJHL as an "outlaw" league. "We preferred to call it *independent*," said Munro.

In 1968, Munro left Estevan to rescue the floundering Calgary Centennials, a junior team that was drawing fewer than three hundred fans to its games at the Stampede Corral. He built it into a winning squad that attracted up to six thousand fans during the regular season and more than seven thousand during the playoffs. "Give the fans a good brand of hockey and they'll beat down the doors," declared Munro. "It's the product that counts."

During his first season coaching in Calgary, Munro turned the Centennials from a basement team into a second-place finisher, and over the ensuing six years he saw the team win three division championships and assorted second- and third-place rankings. The stars of his teams included such future NHL stalwarts as Jimmy Watson (who helped the Philadelphia Flyers win two Stanley Cups), John Davidson, Randy Rota, Mike Rogers, and Danny Gare.

Winning teams were important for Munro, but no less important was the development of young hockey players. His efforts in this regard were worthy of the Hall of Fame recognition that he never received. "I don't want to make hockey bums out of these boys," he said. "I want to give them guidance that will make them good citizens."

He left his mark in all the places where he coached. "Scotty was responsible for the credibility of Estevan as a junior hockey city," wrote an Estevan hockey columnist after Munro died in 1975, and the sentiment was echoed in Blairmore and Lethbridge. Nobody in the big-time hockey cities sneered when a young player said he came from small-town Alberta or Saskatchewan and had been coached by Scotty Munro. They knew that Munro was a more accomplished pro than some of the men behind the bench in Chicago and New York.

Munro was just fifty-seven when he died of cancer, after a season when the Calgary Centennials finished in the cellar of the western division. It was the first time a Munro team failed to make the WCJHL playoffs. His failing health was one reason. His temperament was another. "Sometimes Scotty didn't win because he let his heart rule," said a coaching colleague, "but I would swim the Atlantic Ocean for him. He was that great a guy."

At the time of Munro's death, the league was comprised of thirteen teams located in cities from Manitoba to British Columbia. Today the Western Hockey League consists of eighteen teams, including franchises in Oregon and Washington State.

Hall of Fame recognition continues to elude Munro. The only memorial to the coach who revived junior hockey in Calgary is a wall display at the Stampede Corral and a trophy given to the WHL regular season champions. He is still remembered and recognized by the chroniclers of the sport. "One of the great men in the game," wrote contributor Dunc Scott in *Alberta On Ice*, an anthology published a decade after Munro's death. "(Cancer) was one game that you knew Scotty couldn't beat."

Mac Coleman

Poet and librarian

1919–1996

Mac Coleman started writing poetry at age twelve and became accomplished enough to win many literary prizes and see his work published in anthologies and textbooks. He was also a librarian, and for that his name will always occupy a special place in the history of Red Deer. When Coleman started as the city's first and only professional librarian in 1964, Red Deer's public library occupied a tiny space on the second floor of city hall. When he retired nineteen years later, the library had its own building and eight times as much space.

Born on a small dairy farm near Vanguard, Saskatchewan, Coleman worked as a teacher and school principal in various Saskatchewan communities before completing a degree in library science at the University of Toronto in 1947. He landed his first library job in Regina, and then worked as a librarian in Brandon and Calgary before settling in Red Deer at age forty-five with his wife and three children.

In many instances, he combined library work with writing and teaching. When he moved to Calgary in 1960, Coleman lectured in library science at Mount Royal College while also working as the city's assistant chief librarian.

He was a prolific writer. In Brandon, while serving as the city's chief librarian, he wrote a weekly books column for the *Brandon Sun* newspaper and published a history of Brandon titled *Face of Yesterday*. During his four years in Calgary, he wrote a weekly column for the *Albertan* newspaper, reporting on recent acquisitions by the library and offering general news and comment from the world of books. He also published short stories and poetry, led literary discussion groups, and served on a panel advising the provincial government on what it should consider, or not consider, "objectionable literature." In his spare time, the lanky librarian who reminded small children of Dr. Seuss's *Cat in the Hat* character, played golf, tennis, and volleyball.

When Coleman arrived in Red Deer in 1964, he immediately announced that for a 1967 centennial project he would be leading the push to get the library into its own building. He envisaged a facility with films, recordings, art gallery, and auditorium, along with the collections of books and periodicals. Three years later, his project became a reality when the Red Deer Centennial Library opened. Coleman later oversaw such developments as introduction of interlibrary loans and installation of an electronic security system to reduce book theft.

Coleman continued to write while watching over the growth of Red Deer library. He contributed a regular column to the *Red Deer Advocate*, offering whimsical commentary on the tribulations of small-town life as well as keeping readers up-to-date on library activities. His poetry was published in a college textbook, *Demanding Age*, and he won the Alberta Poetry Prize twice. In one of the winning poems, "Bus Ride," he turned a Greyhound trip from Red Deer to Edmonton into a nightmare journey through the dark of a winter night. The driver, he observed, "holds fate and destiny in hands that seem red and swollen as they grasp the wheel."

Coleman retired from the library in 1984, and told the *Advocate* he planned to spend the rest of his life living and writing in his adopted city. He continued to write his newspaper column, using the library as a resource for his deliberations on language and literature, and using his own experiences to enrich his commentaries on prairie winters and his affection for a poodle named Micky.

It was the kind of column you rarely see in big-city newspapers, but are a regular feature of community life in rural towns. Red Deer, while technically a city, was just a provincial town in Coleman's estimation. Even Calgary and Edmonton fell short of achieving city status. "It takes at least a hundred years to make a city," he reasoned. "Calgary and Edmonton are not yet cities but mere aggregations of rural people. In time they might both become cities."

Coleman wrote columns about matters that would resonate with these "aggregations of rural people." In one, he recalled a winter in Vanguard when the temperature dropped to sixty degrees below zero

Celsius, and a cow named Ruby dropped her calf. "We brought the new, still-wet calf into the house and put it in the cellar until it dried out and the weather got warmer."

Coleman continued to write his column until a couple of years before his death, in April 1996 at age seventy-seven. His legacy to the Red Deer library is manifold. "He steered the direction of library development in Red Deer," said a board member. "We saw tremendous growth in the years Mac was here." The board continues to build on his foundation. His legacy to other libraries in the province includes three collections of short stories beginning with the words, "Once Upon ..."

Joe Shoctor

Lawyer, real estate developer,
and theatre producer

1922–2001

In the early 1960s, Edmonton theatre fans referred to him scornfully as "Broadway Joe" because Joe Shoctor took the proceeds from his lucrative law practice and real estate investments and spent them co-producing plays in New York. However, when he founded the Citadel Theatre in 1965—and thus gave Edmonton the only professional theatre between Winnipeg and Vancouver—they hailed him as the man who made flowers bloom in the desert.

Without Shoctor, professional theatre in Edmonton would never have evolved the way it did. The Edmonton Fringe Festival is just one of the many events to flower as a result of his trail-blazing efforts as an audience builder. His initiatives are commonly seen as responsible for the growth of dozens of spin-off theatre companies and a highly regarded theatre program at the University of Alberta. With Shoctor's Citadel at the centre of a ring of satellite theatres, Edmonton today boasts more theatres per capita than any other North American centre.

His theatrical bent was evident early. Edmonton-born Shoctor was the son of an immigrant Russian street peddler who sold second-hand goods from a stall located where the Edmonton Art Gallery now stands. Shoctor produced and directed variety shows while attending Victoria Composite High School and wrote its school song. He performed as a comedian and as a song-and-dance man. By the time he completed a law degree at the University of Alberta in the early 1940s, Shoctor was convinced he was destined for a career in show business. He went to Hollywood thinking he might act in films, but was told by casting agents that he didn't have the right look for leading roles.

After playing a few small roles at theatres in California, Shoctor returned to Edmonton to practise law, make some money, and try to get into show business on his own terms. "I didn't have the guts to struggle," he said. "I just wasn't prepared to starve and suffer for my craft." He continued to do some acting and directing while building up his law practice and growing rich on real estate investments. He also served as a local impresario for such touring acts as the Happy Gang, Johnny Otis, and the Ink Spots.

As his business interests flourished, Shoctor started drifting toward New York where he invested in a few Broadway productions and thought he might eventually establish himself as a full-time producer. However, after losing money on a succession of Broadway flops, Shoctor decided to remain in Edmonton and continue his involvement from afar.

Some Edmontonians didn't like that. One man called an Edmonton radio hot-line show and asked why Shoctor was wasting time trying to make a splash in New York when he might be doing something useful for Edmonton by putting on plays in the Alberta capital.

"That really spurred me," Shoctor said. "He was right—why didn't we do them here?"

With the help of three friends, he bought a run-down Salvation Army building and converted it into a 277-seat theatre for a combined cost of $250,000. This is how the Citadel was born in 1965.

A more cautious promoter might have been daunted by the fact that a previous attempt to start a professional theatre in Edmonton had ended in failure two years previously. Shoctor could certainly see that finding professional talent was going to be a challenge for him. "I couldn't get Canadian actors to come from Toronto," he said. "They'd say, 'Oh God—what if I miss a radio commercial?'"

Shoctor hired an American artistic director, John Hulbert of Philadelphia, and launched the first Citadel season with an intentionally controversial production of Edward Albee's *Who's Afraid of Virginia Woolf?*, a corrosive drama about the emptiness of marital relationships. The play got lots of media attention and achieved Shoctor's goal of filling the theatre with curious spectators. However, Edmonton wasn't quite ready to support professional theatre on an ongoing basis.

After a couple of shaky years, marked by weak artistic leadership, no government funding, and low standards, the Citadel finally hit its stride in 1968 with the appointment of Sean Mulcahy, a thirty-six-year-old Irish-born director who announced ambitious plans to turn the Citadel into "another Abbey Theatre." Mulcahy doubled the subscriptions in five years and paved the way for future directors such as Britain's John Neville and Peter Coe to realize Shoctor's dream of making the Citadel "an outpost of Broadway."

This didn't sit well with cultural nationalists who felt Shoctor should be hiring Canadian directors and using his government-subsidized theatre to further the development of Canadian drama. Shoctor, however, wanted his theatre to have an international identity, and he wasn't about to let the nationalists limit his scope. "We're not a regional theatre," he insisted. "We're a theatre of national and international significance."

After an explosion of activity during the 1970s, when the Citadel moved from the old Salvation Army building into an elaborate downtown theatre complex, and attracted wide attention with shows imported from or bound for London and New York, the Citadel started to falter. One reason for this was Shoctor's insistence on exercising his right as executive producer to reject plays that he didn't like. This resulted in frequent clashes with his artistic directors.

Neville left in 1978 to take over Halifax's Neptune Theatre and later become artistic director of the Stratford Festival. His successor Coe quit in 1980 in a dispute with Shoctor over programming. Then came a decade-long creative drought when the Citadel incurred criticism for being the only major regional theatre in Canada to operate without a full-time artistic director. Shoctor was unrepentant about this. "After you've had Neville and Coe, you don't just settle for anyone," he said.

Shoctor served as de facto artistic director himself for part of the 1980s. The Citadel mounted a number of spectacular and costly failures, including musical adaptations of Mordecai Richler's *The Apprenticeship of Duddy Kravitz* and Robert Louis Stevenson's *Treasure Island*. During the same period the Citadel building grew to include five performance spaces and a large indoor park, prompting one Edmonton critic to comment, "The Citadel represents an achievement of real estate more than theatre."

The tide began to turn in 1991 when Shoctor appointed former Stratford Festival director Robin Phillips as artistic director, and the Citadel began to regain national prestige with a series of well-received productions. The success pattern continued into the twenty-first century under directors Duncan McIntosh and Bob Baker, when the Citadel offered a combination of popular main-stage programming, second-stage experimental dramas, educational programs, touring shows, and festivals for young people.

Shoctor, meanwhile, consolidated his reputation as Edmonton's "Mr. Downtown," participating in a number of development initiatives, not all of them associated with theatre. Always an Edmonton booster, he had helped revive the Edmonton Eskimos in 1949 and served as the club's first secretary-manager. He chaired the downtown development committee for five years, and during that period spearheaded such projects as the Jasper Avenue improvements, the Old Town Market development, the establishment of the Edmonton Concert Hall Foundation, and the acquisition of land for Grant MacEwan College. "It's my home," said Shoctor. "It's given me everything I have, and I want to give something back to it."

In July 2000, at age seventy-seven, Shoctor closed his law practice and accepted a volunteer position as a resource person at the theatre that he had founded thirty-five years previously. "I've been the ghost of the operation for a long time," he said. "I'm still with it enough to know what's going on in the theatre world and what the Edmonton public likes."

He died in April 2001, at age seventy-eight, after suffering a heart attack. Premier Ralph Klein was one of the many to acknowledge his contribution: "Great cities are built by people just like Joe Shoctor—people with vision, with humour, and with remarkable abilities."

J. Patrick O'Callaghan

Newspaper publisher

1925–1996

Alberta print journalism has produced a number of intrepid publishers who crusaded fearlessly for freedom of the press. During the 1930s, a group of Alberta publishers, under the leadership of the *Edmonton Journal*'s John M. Imrie, undertook to serve in the role normally assumed by the official Opposition after William Aberhart's Social Credit party gained fifty-six seats in the sixty-three-seat legislature. When Aberhart attempted to muzzle the publishers with a bill titled "An Act to Ensure the Publication of Accurate News and Information," the publishers denounced what they called "the Gag Law" and took the matter to the Supreme Court of Canada. The court ruled in 1938 that the bill was unconstitutional. The Privy Council in England upheld this verdict.

For his leadership in attacking Aberhart's press bill, Imrie was awarded a Pulitzer Prize for special public service. Five other Alberta dailies and ninety weeklies received certificates of merit for the role they had played in the cause of newspaper freedom.

History repeated itself during the 1970s when Peter Lougheed's Conservatives won seventy-four of seventy-nine seats in the Alberta legislature. This time, it was the turn of a maverick *Edmonton Journal* publisher named Jeremiah Patrick O'Callaghan to turn the paper into Alberta's "unofficial opposition." While he didn't have to contend with a press control bill, as his predecessors did in the 1930s, O'Callaghan felt nevertheless that the 1979 election landslide had limited the opportunity for certain viewpoints to be expressed. "There were a lot of people out there who obviously had no voice anymore," he said. "Somebody had to look after the interests of the 50 percent or so of Albertans who had no voice in the Legislature. A daily newspaper, because it had no allegiance to anyone except its readers, could take on that role." Later, he claimed, "We did a pretty good job of keeping the rascals honest, of ensuring that such massive power was never abused. We did it without ever becoming partisan."

O'Callaghan ran three daily newspapers during his thirty years in Alberta journalism. An Irish-born gardener's son from Mallow, County Cork, he moved with his family to England as a child during the depression. He entered the newspaper business when he left school at sixteen to join the weekly *Malton Gazette* in North Yorkshire. He spent three years with the Royal Air Force during the Second World War and resumed his newspaper career in 1947 as a copy editor with the daily *Yorkshire Evening Press*. He married his first wife, Lorna, a nurse who became the mother of their four sons and one daughter. He moved on to the *Yorkshire Evening Post* in Leeds, where he said he received "an extra two guineas a week to cover pigeon racing," and then to the morning *Liverpool Post*. When the *Liverpool Post* and its sister paper, the afternoon *Liverpool Echo*, acquired the *Red Deer Advocate* in 1959, they sent thirty-four-year-old O'Callaghan to Alberta to turn the twice-weekly paper into a daily.

The move suited O'Callaghan. He had always wanted to get away from what he saw as the bleakness of post-war England, and Canada beckoned as a land of opportunity. In Red Deer, he quickly became more than a semi-anonymous name on the editorial page masthead. He wrote front-page editorials under his own photo byline, reminding readers that a resident of their community—not an absentee landlord—was commanding the day-to-day operations of the local paper.

After nine years in Red Deer, O'Callaghan joined the Southam-owned *Edmonton Journal* as assistant to publisher Ross Munro. He then moved around the Southam organization for eight years before returning to Edmonton in 1976 to become publisher of the *Journal*. At that point, he began to show Albertans the kind of advocacy journalism that moved beyond news reporting and editorial commentary to social activism.

When Edmonton city council members met behind closed doors in 1979 and voted themselves a 60 percent pay increase, O'Callaghan did more than have the event covered by the *Journal* as a news story. He launched a personal suit against the councillors and got the raise rolled back.

When federal combines investigators raided his *Journal* office, "seizing many files for unexplained reasons," he went all the way to the Supreme Court of Canada to challenge their right to invade his office. His legal victory there made him the first Canadian to use the Charter of Rights and Freedoms to win an important battle in the Supreme Court.

O'Callaghan encountered some public resistance from *Calgary Herald* editor-in-chief Bill Gold when he declared the *Journal* Alberta's "unofficial opposition." Gold wrote in his *Herald* column that newspapers had "a distinct and useful social role, essential even," but they did not have a direct role to play in the electoral process, "and I think it would be rather dangerous if we did." This marked the beginnings of a feud between O'Callaghan and Gold that came to a head after O'Callaghan was named publisher of the *Herald* in 1982. Gold left a few years later to become editorial director for the competition, the *Calgary Sun*. While Gold did eventually return to the *Herald*, he did so as a political columnist, not as editor-in-chief. O'Callaghan preferred to put his own editorial stamp on the papers he ran.

Though he ran the papers on behalf of owners who lived elsewhere, O'Callaghan carried on as if the papers belonged to him. Fuelled by competition from the tabloid *Calgary Sun* and from the right-wing *Alberta Report* magazine, he worked to make the *Herald* the voice of Alberta. "Politically, we've never had a voice," he explained. "How can we when we only have twenty-one MPs who are swamped in Parliament, and a Senate that's a joke at best. We're totally ignored except when they want something from us. The only weapon we have is our voice."

Politically independent, to the provincial Liberals O'Callaghan seemed like a Conservative; to the Conservatives he seemed more like a New Democrat. At the root of his independence was his passion for preserving the freedom of the press. "We will never surrender our faith in the utmost limits of the public's right to know," he declared. "Nor will we ever stop defending that democratic right to exercise complete editorial freedom, without fear or favour." As president of the Canadian Daily Newspaper Publishers Association, he argued successfully against government intervention in the newspaper

ALBERTA ORIGINALS

industry after the Kent Royal Commission inquiry into newspapers recommended that the print media be regulated like the broadcast industry. "I value freedom of the press too highly ever to want to let that wolf get in the door," said O'Callaghan.

His independence made O'Callaghan a loner. He got no support from Southam's Toronto owners when he thundered in print against the federal National Energy Program, a controversial interventionist policy aimed at increasing Canadian ownership of the oil industry. By his own choice, O'Callaghan remained at arm's length from the Alberta politicians and business leaders who might have become his closest allies. "In this job, sooner or later, someone wants a favour or special treatment," he explained, "so I've avoided terribly close friendships."

His eastern bosses eventually tired of his independence, especially when it started costing them money. He had a penchant for letting profits drop rather than cut the space devoted to news. His bosses recalled him to Toronto to become Southam's first travelling professor of journalism at the end of 1988 when Calgary's automobile dealers started pulling their advertisements from the *Herald* in protest over a series of consumer stories listing suggested retail prices of new vehicles. "A typical swan song for a career that has been studded with a certain amount of controversy," noted O'Callaghan with a certain pride.

He was then sixty-three. Instead of settling into quiet retirement, he and his second wife, Joan Abeles, moved to Aurora, Ontario. Over the next seven years he used his typewriter to pound out a steady stream of freelance columns on Canadian unity, freedom of the press, and other subjects.

His last column appeared in the *Globe and Mail* on Canada Day, 1996, just one month before he succumbed to heart problems at age seventy. The stated subject was Southam's announced decision to establish its own national news service as an alternative to the Canadian Press wire agency. The real subject, however, was something close to O'Callaghan's independent heart. Recalling that the Southam publishers of his era had always been free to back the political party of their choice, O'Callaghan expressed hope the proposed news service would not result in Southam newspapers singing the same political tune across the land. "One would like to think that an element of such independence has survived the various crises Southam has passed through in recent years."

Ralph Scurfield

Home builder and philanthropist

1928–1985

Home builder Ralph Scurfield had three mottoes:
- Build a home as if you were building it for yourself.
- Don't be concerned about being the biggest. Be the best.
- Have only one purpose in life: to serve the community.
  Everything else will follow.

Scurfield followed his own maxims and left some significant markings on the wall. He was a schoolteacher from small-town Manitoba who moved to Alberta in his early twenties, parlayed a talent for carpentry into a successful career as a home builder and gave back to his community by contributing eight million dollars to construct a management faculty building at the University of Calgary.

Scurfield began his building career in Edmonton, where he worked his way up to construction supervisor for McConnell Homes. He moved to Calgary in 1957, and took advantage of an opportunity to buy a 25 percent stake in Nu-West Homes, a small company with a book value of sixty thousand dollars, then building fifty homes a year.

Over a twenty-five-year period, Scurfield built Nu-West into a phenomenally successful multinational conglomerate worth $1.5 billion. He built quality homes in most of Calgary's subdivisions, helped initiate Alberta's new-home warranty program, expanded across Canada and into the United States, and diversified into petroleum and the commercial areas of construction and real estate.

Notwithstanding Scurfield's motto about being the best, not the biggest, it seemed as if Nu-West wanted to be both. The company built thirteen hundred homes across the continent and then moved into the oil patch with the purchase of Voyager Petroleums. Scurfield compared himself, in characteristic Calgary Stampede terms, to a driver in a chuckwagon race. "The horses are going like heck, and so are all the young outriders, while I'm sitting back and trying to hold onto the reins."

As for his motto about serving the community, Scurfield did that too. He volunteered with such organizations as the United Way and the North Hill Businessmen's Association, and bought control of the Calgary Flames when the team had an absentee landlord in the form of Vancouver promoter Nelson Skalbania. Scurfield said it was important to Calgary's stature and development to have an NHL franchise that was locally owned.

His biggest gift to the community was an eight-million-dollar donation toward the construction of the University of Calgary's management faculty building, now named Scurfield Hall. Scurfield had taken advanced management at Harvard when he was in his late forties, and there he saw the value of having a major educational facility that attracted the best and the brightest. He hoped a similar facility in Calgary would prevent the city's best students from taking their talents elsewhere.

The Scurfield gift to the University of Calgary came during 1980 when Nu-West posted a $56.7 million profit. The following year, with no awareness of the looming recession, Scurfield bought the Sunshine Village ski resort for fifteen million dollars. As 1981 came to a close, the huge Nu-West empire began to crumble under the weight of soaring interest rates and economic downturn. By mid-1984, the company was $1.4 billion in debt. It subsequently underwent a restructuring process, was sold to Americans, and metamorphosed into Glenayre Electronics. At the time of his death, Scurfield had stepped aside as chief executive officer, reduced his interest in the company to 4 percent, and was spending more time on the ski slopes than in the office.

He died in a skiing accident at age fifty-seven. An avid sportsman all his life, Scurfield had skied on the riverbanks of Winnipeg while earning science and education degrees at the University of Manitoba, and he particularly liked to ski in secluded wilderness areas high in the mountains where the powder was deep and the views were magnificent.

The fatal accident occurred in British Columbia's Cariboo Mountains above Blue River, 190 kilometres north of Kamloops, during a time, in February 1985, when the avalanche danger was high. Scurfield, who was on a week-long helicopter skiing trip with a group of twelve including his youngest son, died in a snowslide while crossing a steep open slope to return to the helicopter. The cascading snow buried Scurfield within seconds. The avalanche also killed fellow skier Randy Paige Broyhill, the twenty-six-year-old son of a Virginia millionaire.

Two court cases followed. In the first, the British Columbia Supreme Court awarded $1.1 million in damages to his widow, Sonia Scurfield, while ruling that her husband was partly to blame for his death. In the second case, concluded in January 1993, the B.C. Court of Appeal nullified the damage award, and ruled that Scurfield should be held entirely responsible for his death. The disappointed family members talked about appealing to the Supreme Court of Canada, but they never proceeded with that action.

The Alberta Home Builders Association created a memorial award in Scurfield's name, which is given annually to the building firm in the province that best reflects the spirit of Scurfield's Nu-West in its construction activities. Members of the association recall that his success was built on a foundation of always giving the customers what they wanted. "Keep the customers happy," said Scurfield. "The day I quit trying to satisfy customers is the day we should all get out of this business."

Eugene Steinhauer

Pioneer Native broadcaster and
Aboriginal treaty rights advocate

1928–1995

The First Nations of Canada have a timeless oral culture but the world of written language took no note of that before the European settlers arrived in the seventeenth century. For a long time after that, writing about Native life and culture was published mainly by non-Natives in non-Native publications. Up until the 1960s there were virtually no Native writers and no Native-owned publications.

Nor were there any Native broadcasters. As Alberta Native writer Donna Rae Paquette has noted, "We could be ditch diggers and waitresses and chamber maids, we could fight forest fires and clean other people's houses, pick rocks, hoe sugar beets and do the many tedious backbreaking servile types of labour expected of us. But we always knew there was no such thing as a professional Native person, a white-collar Indian."

Eugene Steinhauer helped change this reality. A Cree from the Saddle Lake reserve west of St. Paul, he started out in the mid-1960s with a tape recorder and some simple editing equipment. He began producing Cree-language public affairs and news programs for broadcast by the CBC to the residents of northern Alberta. Within a few years, his one person communications venture had grown into the Alberta Native Communications Society, and the modern era of indigenous Native media had begun to unfold.

Steinhauer was a fourth-generation Albertan. His Ojibwa great-grandfather, Henry Bird Steinhauer, was born with a Native last name that means "southern skies." He received his foster name from a Philadelphia banker who adopted him during the early nineteenth century. Henry Bird was educated in New York and made his mark as the first Canadian Native ordained a Methodist minister. He built his mission, a Christian community for Natives, near Whitefish Lake in what is now northeastern Alberta.

The early history of the Steinhauer family is the story of missionary activity in the Canadian West. Henry Bird opened the first Protestant Church in the Lac La Biche region in 1864, and he was the first to translate the Bible into Cree. His missionary sons, Robert and Egerton, collaborated on a hymnal in Cree syllabics that was published in Toronto in 1920. His daughter, Abigail, married the son of Rev. George McDougall, the pioneering Methodist missionary who died on a buffalo hunt near what is now Calgary.

By the time Eugene was born in 1928, the family focus had shifted from missionary work to farming, politics, and assertion of Native identity. Eugene's older brother, Ralph, born in 1905, was active with the United Farmers of Alberta during the early 1920s and later founded the Indian Association of Alberta. He achieved a high public profile in Alberta during the 1970s when he became the first Native person to serve as a lieutenant-governor. He died in 1987.

Eugene received his education at a residential school and he drifted for some years before finding a focus for himself as a communications pioneer. He saw Native people in Alberta as being without a voice, living in widely separated communities, and largely unaware of one another's activities. With his CBC Radio programs he began to build a network through which information from each reserve could be coordinated for the benefit of all.

The first broadcasts were halting and unpolished, but as writer Donna Rae Paquette noted, "We could finally turn the radio on and listen to one of our people talking about issues that affected our people." To complement the radio programming, Steinhauer founded a monthly newspaper, *The Native People*, and staffed it with people who had no experience but were willing to learn and had something to say.

During the 1970s, Eugene Steinhauer began following in his brother's political footsteps. A shy man, Eugene was reluctant initially to get involved in politics, but there were things that needed to be said publicly about the preservation of Native treaty rights and he wanted to say them. He did so first as chief of the Saddle Lake First Nation for seven years, and then as president of the Indian Association of Alberta. "The Indian people won't be patient forever," he said. "If white people don't listen now, they will have to listen later."

In November 1980, Steinhauer made headlines when he led

against the provincial government one of the largest Native demonstrations that Alberta has ever seen. More than five thousand Natives, representing every band in the province, assembled on the steps of the Legislature to protest what they viewed as the Lougheed government's efforts to keep protection of treaty and aboriginal rights out of the new Canadian constitution. A century of broken treaty promises and unsettled land claims had left Steinhauer with little hope that such traditional rights as Native control over reserve land and resources would be guaranteed by the constitution.

By the end of 1981, Steinhauer's worst fears had been realized. The federal government and nine provinces had voted to remove protection of Native rights from the constitutional package, and Steinhauer was warning of future violence and demonstrations. "Cornered people fight back," he said. "If people feel they have to fight for their lives, they will do so."

In the beginning, the fight was confined to the political arena and to the courts. Steinhauer and his followers pledged support for the provincial NDP in the Alberta election of 1982, claiming the Lougheed government "does not recognize our culture and our heritage." Steinhauer also led delegations of Native leaders to London to launch a series of challenges in the British courts, demanding that the rights of indigenous peoples be entrenched in the Canadian constitution as they were in the British North America Act.

The British High Court refused to hear the constitutional challenge. Lord Denning declared that jurisdiction involving Natives had passed from Westminster to Ottawa in 1867, the year of Confederation. Steinhauer repeated his warning about violence and demonstrations. He said that Alberta Natives would not stand by and let valid treaty rights be eroded.

His anger was deeply felt. It was rooted in Steinhauer's long-held belief that his Native ancestors had surrendered land and resources to the Europeans in return for certain treaty-sanctioned guarantees concerning the preservation of Native lifestyle and culture. Instead of upholding such guarantees, however, the federal government had embarked on a policy of "assimilating" the First Nations into mainstream society—an "alien culture," as Steinhauer called it—without their consent.

During the 1990s, Steinhauer saw his predictions of violence and demonstrations materialize as clashes between Natives and police occurred at such places as Oka and Kahnawake in Quebec, Camp Ipperwash in Ontario, Gustafsen Lake in British Columbia, and the Oldman River in southern Alberta. Steinhauer died in 1995 at age sixty-seven, still unhappy about the assimilation policy that had made his people feel like shattered glass in the Canadian mosaic.

Jimmy Fitzsimmons

Jockey

1929–2001

In Calgary, champion horse riders generally tend to be rodeo riders or show jumpers. Jimmy Fitzsimmons achieved excellence in a different sphere of equine endeavour, as a racehorse jockey. Starting at the relatively late age of twenty-one, he rode to success as one of Canada's top jockeys of the 1960s, twice winning the nation's greatest race, the Queen's Plate.

The son of an Irish coal miner, Fitzsimmons grew up in the Bankview district of Calgary when it was still pasture. His first involvement with horses involved buying colts from the local Natives, breaking them, and selling them for a profit.

An accident as a toddler paved the way for his future success as a jockey. The family's Irish setter wrapped its leash around him, throwing little Jimmy to the ground, and breaking his leg. "After that, I never grew much bigger." When he grew to adulthood he was just five feet tall.

Though he spent a lot of time at the track as a youngster, and learned to ride before he was a teenager, Fitzsimmons didn't embark on a career in racing silks until it was almost too late. At age twenty-one he left his job as an apprentice machinist and signed up with Calgary racehorse trainer Cap Miller as an apprentice jockey. He was beyond the prescribed "twenty-one and under" age limit for starting apprentices, but a sympathetic racing commission judge agreed to look at the contract with his "blind eye."

The apprenticeship contract, Fitzsimmons said later, was "like a slave agreement." He had to "clean the stables, brush down the horses, walk them, feed them, gallop them and sleep with them in the barns." It was a hard life "but I got room and board, clothing and twenty dollars a month." The experience, he said, taught him respect and "how to appreciate what I had."

He rode his first race in Edmonton on 13 July 1951, and

registered his first win thirteen days later in Saskatoon aboard a mount named Alaska. By season's end he had nineteen wins to his credit.

Fitzsimmons piloted fifty horses to victory in 1952. Pleased with his success, he bought back his contract from trainer Cap Miller for thirty-five hundred dollars and hit the summer racing circuit as a freelance jockey. He moved to Toronto in 1953 but didn't have much luck there and returned to Calgary at the end of the season. In 1954, his career almost ended at Calgary's Victoria Park when his horse fell and Fitzsimmons suffered a fractured skull and broken collarbone. After a long period of convalescence, however, he returned to the track and was named Western Canada's leading rider in 1957 with seventy-one victories. Then he hit a three-year slump.

Fitzsimmons moved back to Toronto in 1960. He did well enough to be signed as a contract rider for Windfields Farms, a successful thoroughbred operation owned by businessman E. P. Taylor. After that, Fitzsimmons scored some of his greatest victories. He was the leading sweepstakes rider in Ontario between 1961 and 1963.

In June 1962, Fitzsimmons became the first rider from Western Canada to win the Queen's Plate, the oldest continuously run sweepstakes in North America. The Queen Mother made the presentation, and Fitzsimmons was delighted to discover that she shared his love of horses. "She told me she hoped to see me ride some day at Epsom."

Fitzsimmons had one of his most memorable riding experiences in 1963 when he rode the legendary Northern Dancer to victory in the Carleton Stake in Toronto. It was Northern Dancer's last race in Canada before being moved to New York, where Taylor stabled and trained any of his horses that showed world-class potential. In 1964, Northern Dancer became the first Canadian-bred horse to win the Kentucky Derby and then went on to win the Preakness and finish third in the Belmont.

Fitzsimmons won the Queen's Plate for the second time in 1967, then retired from horseracing in 1970 at age forty-one. He later returned to Calgary where he maintained his association with the track by working at Stampede Park as a clerk of scales and as a timer for the harness races. He was inducted into the Canadian Horse Racing Hall of Fame in 1984. Over the course of his nineteen-year career, he had scored 1,380 victories. Northern Dancer was also inducted into the Hall of Fame in 1984. Fitzsimmons recalled that the horse had been overweight and out of shape because of a hoof injury in 1963, yet still coasted to victory in the Carleton Stake. "I decided to just whack him a couple to clear the field, and bingo, we were on top right now."

Fitzsimmons took compulsory retirement from Stampede Park in 1994, at age sixty-five. A few months beforehand, he had told a reporter, "I won't retire till I'm forced. I'd go crazy if I didn't have the track to go to. That's my home." He died in March 2001 at age seventy-one. To the end of his life, he maintained his 105-pound riding weight.

Violet King Henry

Lawyer and civil rights activist

1930–1981

The history of blacks in Alberta is the story of a small group of immigrants who have overcome discrimination and adversity to take advantage of the opportunities of Canadian life and make notable contributions to society.

Exemplifying this is the story of Violet King Henry, a railway worker's daughter who went to law school with Peter Lougheed, who later became Alberta's premier. In 1953, Henry became the first black law student to graduate from the University of Alberta. The following year, she became the first black woman to practise law in Canada when she was admitted to the bar in Calgary.

Whenever the story of black achievement in Alberta is told, it rarely includes more than a passing reference to Henry. The story always seems to be dominated by the achievement of John Ware, a legendary nineteenth century cowboy from South Carolina whose stature in the Alberta ranching community became such that his log home was preserved as a museum, and his name given to a Millarville park, a creek, and a Calgary junior high school.

Ware looms large in Alberta myth because he rates co-billing in the history books as a contemporary of the mounted police, the missionaries, and the other pioneers of the frontier era. He is the only black to make the list. For several years after Ware's death in 1905, the story of black achievement in Alberta went largely unreported in the mainstream press. One reason for this is that the newspapers in Calgary and Edmonton had no real liking for the fugitive slaves who fled oppression and segregation in the American south and came north to seek a better life. The press, in point of fact, wanted to keep Alberta white. "The influx of Negro settlers promises to have a disastrous influence on the welfare and development of this fair province," said one Calgary newspaper. "They are not adapted to the country and are not a desirable class of citizens."

The first wave of black immigration to Alberta, between 1908 and 1911, was also, for many years, the last wave. More than eight hundred black refugees moved north of Edmonton, to the Athabasca region, to take up homesteads. About two hundred more settled in the Edmonton-area farming communities of Wildwood, Breton, and Campsie. Three hundred more settled in the cities of Edmonton and Calgary. All told, in 1911, blacks comprised about one-third of 1 percent of the Alberta population. That was too much as far as some people were concerned. "Negroes are not wanted in Alberta," declared the *Calgary Albertan* newspaper in May 1911. "Many most desirable white settlers have been deterred from settling in the country."

This backlash against blacks occurred just eight years after the Canadian government started encouraging American blacks to move north, placing advertisements in American newspapers saying, "No better opportunity affords itself to the agricultural Negro than in Western Canada." In 1911, the Calgary and Edmonton boards of trade both passed resolutions urging the federal government to "effectually prevent the advent of Negroes to Western Canada," and to segregate existing black homesteaders, "in a certain defined area or areas from which white settlers should be removed."

While such opposition was isolated and short-lived, it was, in the words of black Calgary writer Cheryl Foggo, "cool enough for them to want to hang together." The federal Liberals never went so far as to introduce actual legislation barring further immigration by American blacks, because that would have alienated both the American government and the black voters in eastern Canada. Through various deterrent strategies—including the hiring of agents to travel to Oklahoma for the express purpose of discouraging black immigrants—the government kept other blacks from entering Canada. The black population of Alberta remained steady at around one thousand from 1911 until the mid-1960s, when blacks from the West Indies and from Africa started arriving in Alberta in great numbers.

Violet King Henry's parents were among the first group of black immigrants from Kansas and Oklahoma who came to Alberta before the First World War. They homesteaded with their families in the

Breton area southwest of Edmonton, but found the farming difficult because the soil was not suitable for grain and the nearest elevator, in Leduc, was a three-day wagon ride away. Eventually they moved to Calgary. Violet's father, John R. King, became a railway porter, and her mother, Stella, worked as a seamstress.

One of four children, Violet grew up in the inner city, Hillhurst-Sunnyside district of Calgary, graduated from Crescent Heights High, and completed a business course ("always one for having her head in a book," said her mother) while waiting for her eighteenth birthday and admission to the University of Alberta. An accomplished musician, Violet covered her university tuition and living expenses with the money she earned from teaching classical piano. After distinguishing herself at university as a student who made outstanding contributions to campus life through her volunteer work with the students' union and the student housing committee, she graduated with a combined arts and law degree. She articled with Calgary lawyer Edward J. McCormick, and practised law in Calgary for a few years before moving to Ottawa to work for the federal citizenship branch.

After seven years in Ottawa, Violet moved at age thirty-nine to Newark, New Jersey, to take what her mother called a "needful" position with the YM-YWCA, helping qualified black job applicants land employment at companies that only wanted to hire whites. Violet did so well in that job that the Y gave her its Special Mott Fellowship for her "outstanding record of accomplishments." The fellowship took her to Chicago to study urban renewal programs for blacks, after which she worked for the Y in Chicago. In 1976, she became the first woman to be named to a senior management position with the American national executive of the Y. Calgary's *Albertan* newspaper referred to her proudly as "Calgary's beloved former barrister."

Violet King Henry was just fifty-one when she died of cancer in 1981. "This outstanding Alberta woman, a first in so many ways, had her illustrious career cut short," wrote Phyllis Johnson in *The Window of our Memories*, a 1990 publication by the Black Cultural Research Society of Alberta. "However, she made her mark on this world."

A few years before her daughter's death, Violet's mother, Stella, said she hoped her daughter's civil rights work on behalf of fellow blacks would inspire white employers to become more tolerant. "I don't know why they can't take people as people instead of worrying about their colour." Violet King Henry was one who tried to make it so.

Les Kimber

Film producer

1932–1998

Hollywood discovered Alberta after the First World War as a place with an infinite variety of scenic locations where a movie could be shot for next to nothing. It wasn't until the 1970s, however, that the province became a production centre for the motion picture industry, with more to offer than a diversity of scenery, horses, and cowboy and cowgirl extras. One reason was the Alberta Film Commission. In 1972, it was a first of its kind in North America, when it was established to attract film and television business to the province. The other reason was Les Kimber, one of the first Albertans to make a full-time living in film production in his home province.

With a gold chain around his neck, glasses atop his bald head, and an ever-present cigar in his ashtray, Kimber, in his fifties, looked like the stereotypical Hollywood mogul. That was as close as he ever wanted to get to the American capital of the movie business. "I wouldn't give anything to work there," he said. "My stomping grounds is Western Canada, and I love it here. The older I get, the more I appreciate it." Working in Hollywood meant working in a studio. Working in Alberta meant being in the outdoors, where the badlands of the Drumheller Valley could masquerade as the Old West. Kimber liked to look out his office window toward the Rocky Mountains and say, "That's my Hollywood out there."

His work occasionally took him to Los Angeles, where he made the deals that resulted in movie productions coming to Alberta, but he always came back to Calgary, where he was born and raised during the Great Depression. A movie enthusiast from childhood, Kimber decided early on to make his career in show business. "Mainly I was going into television, I thought." He trained in television production in Oregon and Toronto, worked during the early 1960s with Calgary's CFCN Television, and then moved into theatre as a stage actor. He toured North America with bus-and-truck versions of such Broadway musicals as *My Fair Lady* and *The Pajama Game*. He then moved over to the technical side of the theatre business, and eventually returned to Calgary as producer and stage manager for the two semi-professional companies that evolved into Theatre Calgary in 1968.

The financial rewards in theatre were miniscule. Kimber worked fourteen-hour days and made less in a year than he would later make in one day as a film producer. He loved what he was doing, though, "and it all helped my career when I went into the picture business."

Kimber's film break came in 1969 when he was hired as manager of Canadian production for Arthur Penn's *Little Big Man*, a western movie about the events leading up to Custer's Last Stand, much of which was shot around Calgary. Kimber recalled winter temperatures of twenty degrees below zero Celsius when the film was being shot, and said that gave the film a gritty authenticity. "That's what people want to see—reality," he said. "It's not nice everyplace. Everyplace is not Los Angeles."

The 1970s were good for movies in Alberta, mainly thanks to Kimber's lobbying efforts in Los Angeles with Chuck Ross, then the province's film development officer. Movies shot in the province during that period included Robert Altman's *Buffalo Bill and the Indians*, the Canadian film *Why Shoot the Teacher*, Michael Ritchie's *Prime Cut*, and Arthur Hiller's *Silver Streak*, a film about the train that runs from Los Angeles to Chicago. "We could not get the co-operation of the American railroads and that brought us to Canada," said Hiller. "We were eternally grateful, because instead of going to five different states, we simulated five different states in Alberta."

Between movies, Kimber drove gravel trucks and sold cars. He told his auto dealer boss, "When a movie comes, I'm going to be gone. So one came and I went. When I went back he didn't want to hire me any more. And I was the second top salesman there too."

As time went on, Kimber didn't have to sell cars any more. "It took a lot of perseverance and a lot of hanging in there. You've got to pay your dues in this business to make it work." He looked after local production arrangements and loved the challenge of getting whatever the Hollywood directors needed to do their work in Alberta.

For *Superman I*, Kimber had to come up with the cave where the hero lives as a teenager. "We found it behind the glaciers in the Columbia Icefield. We helicoptered in there and found it." For John Frankenheimer's *The Fourth War*, he had to truck in armoured cars from Los Angeles and comb the world for Soviet army uniforms. For *Superman III*, he had to find a gas refinery plant that could be blown up with explosives. "Now where in the world are you going to be allowed to do that? Well, we were able to do it here in Alberta, with the co-operation of the Turbo people and the people in the government."

One of his toughest production challenges was Terrence Malick's *Days of Heaven*, with its plague of locusts and burning grasslands. "We called it *Days of Heaven, Nights of Hell*," said Kimber, but the effort paid off with an Academy Award for best photography. "That was very satisfying."

Among producers and directors throughout North America and the United Kingdom, Kimber was rated one of the best in his field. He had a reputation for keeping movie budgets on track by cutting corners without sacrificing quality. He didn't receive much local recognition for this, but he viewed that as being typically Canadian. "I don't worry about that any more. If you make your name in this business, you make it worldwide and people know who you are. If you can meet their expectations and provide what they want, you do well."

Kimber maintained he was never in the movie business for the money, though the business did bring him a few Cadillacs, a twenty-acre ranch home west of Calgary, a second home in Vancouver, and more money than he needed on which to retire. He would never say how much he was worth. "Who knows? I haven't counted lately. Let's say I'm not fading away to nothing."

He did try retiring in his early fifties after a near-fatal encounter with lymphatic cancer, but returned to the business when his health improved. He worked steadily during the 1990s as production manager on such shows as the *Lonesome Dove* and *North of 60* television series, the made-for-television movie *Sweet Redemption*, and the Disney movie *Noah*. Belated recognition came during this period when Kimber received the 1993 David Billington Award, presented by the Alberta Motion Picture Industries Association for career achievement and contribution to the provincial film business.

Kimber worked until shortly before his death at age sixty-six in November 1998. His last project was *Noah*, a contemporary retelling of the biblical story of Noah's Ark.

Joe Kryczka

Judge and hockey enthusiast

1935–1991

In April 1972, Canadian and Soviet negotiators agreed in Prague to re-establish sports contact between the two countries with an eight-game hockey series. A flamboyant lawyer and hockey players' agent named Alan Eagleson—who was later jailed for fraud relating to misappropriation of player pension funds—attained most of the publicity and credit by being the first to phone the news home to Canada. However, those who took part in the Prague negotiations agreed that the central figure in Canada's success in this endeavour was a Calgary judge and lifelong hockey fan named Joe Kryczka.

Justice Joe, as his friends called him, was a coalminer's son from the Crowsnest Pass who learned his hockey playing defence in the unheated rinks of Blairmore and Coleman. He was, by his own admission, "the worst hockey player" of three brothers. He played for three years with the University of Alberta's Golden Bears hockey team while completing a law degree during the 1950s, and then moved over to the administrative side of the hockey business.

During the 1960s, Kryczka was active as an executive with the Alberta Amateur Hockey Association and the Canadian Amateur Hockey Association (CAHA), eventually serving as president of both. In legal circles, he practised civil and corporate law with a Calgary firm that had future premier Peter Lougheed as one of its senior partners.

In his capacity as president of the CAHA, Kryczka became Canada's chief negotiator during the 1972 talks in Prague that led to a long-awaited series of games between the best hockey teams that Canada and the Soviets could put on the ice. Two years previously, Canada had exited the world hockey stage in a dispute with the International Ice Hockey Federation (IIHF) over the eligibility of professional players. The teams of amateurs that Canada was required to select under IIHF rules had proved no match for the

Soviets in international competition, so Canada withdrew from the IIHF until the basis of eligibility was reduced simply to a player's nationality.

By 1972, the federal government was eager to resolve the international hockey impasse as part of an overall foreign policy initiative aimed at strengthening bilateral relations between Canada and the Soviet Union. After a series of high-level meetings between Canadian and Soviet diplomats and government officials, Kryczka and his negotiating team had the opportunity to try and persuade IIHF members that Canada should re-enter the international hockey arena with "unrestricted" teams of professional players.

The meeting in Prague lasted for three days, and according to Canadian government official Lou Lefaive, Kryczka acquitted himself admirably in the negotiations. Lefaive referred to him admiringly as Canada's "secret weapon" because Kryczka never tipped his hand that he knew the Russian language. He had spoken Russian in the home with his Polish parents as a child and still remembered enough of the language to understand what the Soviet negotiators were saying. He didn't say anything to them about this, however, and did his talking through an interpreter. It was only when the negotiations were concluded, and Canada won the right to select a team of professionals for the Canada-Soviet series, that Kryczka confided to the Soviets that he knew the language.

The announcement of the Canada-Soviet series was greeted with jubilation by Canadian hockey fans, and Eagleson was quick to claim the credit for orchestrating the event. He had not been part of Kryczka's negotiating team, and he had not attended the meetings in Prague. Nevertheless, Eagleson managed to convince Canadians that he was the hero of the hour because he had spent the previous three years promoting the idea of North American professionals playing Europe's top hockey teams.

Kryczka did receive some public acknowledgement for his efforts in landing the hockey series when he was named Canada's sports executive of the year for 1972, but wider recognition was slow in coming. He returned to Calgary and continued working for the cause of his favourite sport. "I still think I can contribute something valuable to the hockey community," he said.

In 1978, at age forty-three, Kryczka was diagnosed with cancer. After a year of treatment, he was philosophical. "I suppose the end result was that I learned to appreciate that nobody is invincible," he said. "Nobody is indispensable." Two years later, he was appointed to the Alberta Court of Queen's Bench. People began to call him Justice Joe.

During the 1980s, Kryczka was in the headlines as the presiding judge in an internationally publicized child custody case involving a seven-year-old boy, Jason Read. The boy's father, an English-born immigrant to Canada, kept Jason in Calgary in defiance of a British court order granting custody to the mother in England. Kryczka directed that the boy remain in Calgary with his father, reasoning that it might be harmful for the boy to return to England with his mother. The Alberta Court of Appeal disagreed and returned the boy to his mother. However, a year later, a British judge ruled that the boy should go back to his father in Canada because the mother was refusing to submit to access orders.

During this same period, Justice Joe was quietly involved in another sporting endeavour, playing a key role with the team that successfully brought the 1988 Olympic Winter Games to Calgary. For his work on that project, and for his lifelong involvement in hockey, he was named to the Canada Sports Hall of Fame in 1990. "A true builder of hockey in Canada at every level," said the accompanying citation. Kryczka said it was nice to be finally recognized for the role that he played in the 1972 series because "I didn't always get the credit."

The Sports Hall of Fame recognition came during the last year of Kryczka's life. The renaming of a Calgary community rink, after years of city hall delay, as the Justice Joe Kryczka Arena came the same year. "Finally, a tribute to the judge," said the headline in a Calgary newspaper in December 1990. Less than a month afterward, the popular judge was dead of cancer at age fifty-five.

Kryczka was never named to the Hockey Hall of Fame, which did recognize Eagleson and others involved in organizing hockey games between European teams and the NHL. In 1997, Kryczka's supporters tried unsuccessfully to have him posthumously inducted into the Hall of Fame. They tried again in early 1998, after Eagleson resigned from the Hall of Fame in the wake of his convictions for fraud, but still to no avail. The honour that eluded Kryczka during his lifetime continues to elude him.

Harold Hanen

Architect and urban designer

1935–2000

While they might not know the name Harold Hanen, Calgarians who live and work downtown are undoubtedly aware of his legacy. They tip their hats to him every time the temperature drops to minus twenty. Harold Hanen was the father of Calgary's Plus-15 system, a heated indoor skywalk development that—at twelve kilometres in length—is presently the most extensive above-ground pedestrian network in the world.

As well as being his lasting contribution to the winter comfort of Calgarians, the Plus-15 walkway system was also a reflection of Hanen's lifelong philosophy. He believed that so-called "winter cities"—defined as having an average January temperature of zero degrees Celsius—should acknowledge, celebrate, and plan for the reality that their citizens can spend up to six months or more annually living with cold and snow.

Hanen designed the Plus-15 system, so-named because the walkways are built fifteen feet above the ground, during the three years he worked for the City of Calgary as a planner in the 1960s. Born and raised in Calgary, he studied fine arts at McGill University before apprenticing in the United States with Frank Lloyd Wright, the eccentric and flamboyant American architect whose efforts to create an indigenous American architecture devoid of European influences impressed the young Calgarian.

Founder of the so-called "prairie-house" school of architecture, Wright believed that urban design should create a natural, organic link between humans and their environment. In contrast to crowded urban Europe, America was a land of wide-open spaces and Wright said that American architecture should reflect the frontier environment. Hanen studied with Wright at the architect's winter retreat in the foothills of the McDowell Mountains near Scottsdale, Arizona, then completed further studies in architecture and urban planning in Boston, Rhode Island, and Philadelphia.

Returning to Calgary in 1966, Hanen joined the city planning department, where he was happy to see that plans were actually put to use rather than shelved. However, he ran into some opposition to his plan for a system of overhead walkways linking downtown buildings. Critics of the plan said it would rob Calgary's downtown streets of vitality. Nevertheless, he did see the system finally implemented in 1969. The first Plus-15 walkway, built at a cost of one hundred thousand dollars, connected what is now the Westin Hotel to a small shopping plaza across the street on Fourth Avenue S.W. Hanen won the Vincent Massey Award for Merit in Urban Planning for his concept.

Hanen left the planning department under a cloud in 1969, dismissed by the mayor and city commissioners for allegedly holding a directorship in a local trust company. He successfully sued for wrongful dismissal and collected $7,350 in lost wages. But it was a Pyrrhic victory because after that, whenever Hanen's firm tried to work on a development project in Calgary, it ran into difficulties at city hall. Because he was now effectively unable to work in Calgary, Hanen began concentrating on projects outside the city, and developed downtown plans for Jasper, Fort McMurray, Kamloops, and Okotoks. He also did design studies for community centres in northern Alberta and for resource centres geared to serve people with physical disabilities.

In 1978, Hanen came in from the cold—as he characterized it— and joined forces with Toronto architect Raymond Moriyama. They began to develop a design concept for a five-block civic square development in downtown Calgary that was to be built at a cost of more than $233 million. The five-block plan was eventually rejected as too grandiose—the city opted for a scaled-down municipal building instead. However, the design scheme allowed Hanen to show Calgarians how he would integrate a major urban development into the foothills landscape as his mentor Frank Lloyd Wright might have done.

Hanen continued to work in Calgary during the 1980s and 1990s, primarily on the restoration of heritage buildings. "It may appear that Calgary is a cut-out cardboard city," he said, "but it's especially important for the young people to see the past. Without the past, there's no continuity." To remind himself of the city's past he located his downtown office in a turn-of-the-century commercial development built by one of early Calgary's leading citizens, Sir James Lougheed. One of Hanen's restoration projects was the Clarence Block, named after one of Lougheed's four sons.

Another focus of Hanen's life during this period was his involvement in the international winter-cities movement, founded in Toronto in 1985 by construction magazine publisher Jack Royale. "Life is about choices," said Hanen. "We winter citizens have a choice: We can let weather rule, inhibit or restrain us, or we can design our communities not only to enhance our geography and our daily lives, but our very sense of selves." He believed that unless winter communities learned to deal with their climatic diversity and extremes, they would never be a force in the global community, either culturally or economically.

He pointed to the Plus-15 system as one innovative response to winter. Other Canadian examples included the invention of the snowmobile and the winter recreational facilities in Banff National Park. "And where would we be without the skiing, figure skating, curling and hockey?" Standing on guard for snowstorms, wind chill, and ice pellets shaped the Canadian character, he said. "People romping in paradise are different from people who have to deal with the unexpected."

Hanen was not entirely pleased with the way his Plus-15 concept evolved as it became an accepted part of life in downtown Calgary. Every new construction project in the commercial core was required by bylaw to join the system, and each development was allowed to put its own creative stamp on the system. However, the overall result, in Hanen's view, was a somewhat characterless network of glass and steel skywalks rather than the dynamic streetscape that he envisaged. Instead of evolving into a place where people would gather for a while, sip coffee, and talk about life and art, it became a linked series of impersonal pedestrian tunnels where the emphasis was on moving from A to B.

"He felt it should be a much more dynamic part of our city, it shouldn't be another street," said his widow, Maria Eriksen, in October 2000 after Hanen died of cancer at age sixty-four. However, for many downtown Calgarians, grateful to be out of the cold as they navigate their way from workplace to restaurant to shopping plaza, the Plus-15 system is not just another street. It is the first step toward living the good life in a winter city.

Ray Lowry

Engineer, scientist, and social activist

1942–2000

In his professional life, Ray Lowry made his mark as an electrical engineer, specializing in the application of radar systems to mapping and environmental problems. However, it was as a social activist pushing for an end to world poverty and hunger that he made what some regard as his greatest contribution. As one of his colleagues said, Lowry believed one of his principal jobs in life was to "leave the campsite cleaner than I found it."

Born near Biggar, Saskatchewan—home of the famous sign that proclaims, "New York is Big, but this is Biggar"—Lowry grew up on a farm and dreamed of working in electronics. His father had dreamed of doing the same thing, but was unable to do so because of the Great Depression and other complicating factors. Lowry trained initially as an electronics technician, but when he saw that the engineers were the ones making the money he decided he wanted to be there too. He earned his bachelor of science degree in electrical engineering at the University of Saskatchewan and—without stopping to get his master's degree—vaulted right into a Ph.D. program at London's Imperial College of Science and Technology, sometimes described as the MIT of England.

"He did this under an Athlone Fellowship which, at the time, was the most prestigious fellowship that a Canadian engineering student could get," said his friend and colleague John Whittaker, professor of engineering management at the University of Alberta.

Lowry completed his Ph.D. in electrical engineering in 1971. He returned to Canada, and as a research scientist, joined the Defence Research Board in Ottawa, where he worked on radar mapping for Arctic applications. In 1975, he moved to the Canada Centre for Remote Sensing. Three years later, he went to work for Intera Technologies where he participated in the development and operation of airborne radar mapping systems.

He wore his credentials lightly. "Most folks never knew that Ray was a Ph.D.," said his friend Cathy Little. "He was far more interested in talking to people to see what they were passionate about, and encouraging them to get on with life."

Little befriended Lowry shortly after Intera transferred him to Calgary in 1983, and together they worked on projects aimed at eradicating world hunger. He saw poverty first-hand when his radar-mapping work took him to remote regions in the developing world, and he vowed to do something about it. He noted a profound irony in the fact that the will to develop new technologies was stronger in North America than the will to save millions of children from dying of largely preventable malnutrition and disease.

In Calgary in 1986, Lowry founded the first Canadian branch of RESULTS, an international network of grassroots action groups dedicated to ending hunger, eliminating poverty, and changing the world for the better. He told his children, daughter Phoebe and son Bevis, they were fortunate to be living in a part of the world that offered them many advantages.

"He said I shouldn't feel guilty about this, but that I should take responsibility for giving something back to improve the world," said Phoebe. He didn't say this in a "preachy way," added Phoebe. Lowry taught by example, showing his children that a person could achieve good things by tackling each of life's projects—even housework—with enthusiasm, energy, determination, and an irrepressible sense of groan-provoking humour. "He made awful, awful puns," explained Phoebe. "The rule was: Don't laugh, it encourages him."

Lowry's work with RESULTS showed that one person could make a difference. One person could write a letter to a politician or to a newspaper asking that the political system be accountable and responsible for ending hunger and poverty. Lowry wrote many letters. His signature appeared frequently on correspondence published in the local newspapers. "It is time for a Team Canada approach to the elimination of poverty," he wrote in January 1997. His proposed solution was simple and innovative: Instead of using traditional, government-to-government foreign aid programs to help the poor, Canada should provide small sums to individual families through a loan system known as microcredit.

The microcredit system was pioneered in Bangladesh in 1978, and has since spread worldwide. In 1998, Canada began operating a microcredit program through the Canadian International Development Agency. Loans averaging less than one hundred dollars each, mostly given to women, have helped millions work their way out of poverty. In a typical example, a poor woman in India borrowed money to buy a milk cow. Within ten months she had repaid the loan and was on her way to becoming self-sufficient. "Empowerment will always trump charity," said Lowry.

He wrote his last letters in the months leading up to his death in November 2000. One of them praised International Co-operation Minister Maria Minna for committing ten million dollars to train teachers in Kosovo. "This is aid that makes it possible for the poor to end their poverty," wrote Lowry.

His death left his RESULTS colleagues determined to carry on his work as a social activist. "We will keep his flame alive by growing our group larger than ever as we move towards our goal of eradicating hunger and absolute poverty from the face of this planet," said Cathy Little.

Winnie Tomm

Academic and mother

1944–1995

Winnie Tomm was a hard-working scholar and academic who left her mark professionally as founding coordinator of the University of Alberta's women's studies program. She was also a wife and mother—for a time, a full-time homemaker—and that aspect of her life was as important to her as any other. Raising her two daughters was a satisfying and enriching experience, she said. Like many stay-at-home mothers, however, she found it difficult to deal with the cultural emphasis on workplace achievement that left women unable to publicly celebrate motherhood as an empowering experience. "Disempowering attitudes toward women in the home range from mild patronization to unequivocal derogation."

Tomm wanted to shout out with joy when her daughters were born in the 1960s. "I felt as though I was eighteen feet in the air, as though I had done something completely miraculous." But she couldn't share her joy as she would have liked. "One of the saddest things is you don't feel legitimate talking about childbirth in many places because most people do not take birth as a significant topic. So people do not hear how women feel so powerful when they give birth. It is magnificent."

Tomm raised her daughters while simultaneously pursuing an eclectic academic career encompassing a wide variety of interests. Born in Medicine Hat and raised in the Cypress Hills of southern Alberta, she studied nursing before her marriage in 1963, at age nineteen, to Calgary psychiatrist Karl Tomm. Over the following two decades, she pursued degree courses in sociology, anthropology, philosophy, and religious studies leading to her doctorate in 1984.

She continued with post-doctoral studies at the University of Calgary's Humanities Institute, taught courses at the university, and always found time to look after the private matters that were important to her. She valued this time spent supporting her busy husband, raising funds for her daughters' extracurricular activities, hiking in the mountains, and playing racquetball with her friends. Women's private lives could not be easily separated from their public lives, she said. "A positive consequence is that women usually stay more connected to their families than men do. Men more often sink into a quiet desperation of loneliness because of their patterns of separating their private and public activities."

Tomm was appointed women's studies coordinator at the University of Alberta in 1988. She moved to Edmonton and spent the next six years commuting back and forth to Calgary. This meant being separated physically from her family, but she was never separated emotionally. When an Edmonton newspaper reporter called her in her capacity as a women's issues expert for an article on childbirth, Tomm was happy to talk about what she called her own "glorious experience" twenty years previously when her daughters were born. By sharing the experience, she said, a woman could reclaim her power as a full and equal shaper of society.

Tomm saw the field of women's studies as "a way for women to understand their lives, cut through myths they have been fed, and get rid of contradictions in their lives." Among those contradictions was the notion that a child born out of wedlock was "illegitimate." If the mother were seen as a person in her own right, her child would be born free of the social stigma of illegitimacy, "which depends on the patriarchal construction of children belonging primarily to fathers."

Her easy manner and shrewd sense of humour served to disarm the skeptics among her colleagues who could see little merit in having women's studies as a separate university discipline. Her humour masked some serious concerns about issues such as sexism in society and the widespread abuse of women and children, which Tomm saw as being closely associated with their lack of social privileges. "Restricting privileges reinforces prejudices against the already underprivileged."

Tomm ran the University of Alberta's women's studies program during a time when the university weathered such incidents as a female engineering student being publicly mocked in an engineering-week skit after she complained about sexism in the engineering faculty. Tomm responded to the incident by meeting with both sides and encouraging dialogue between them. "She was a very good mediator," said a colleague.

She was also a lifelong learner, who taught herself the Tibetan language so she could study the works of a fourth-century Buddhist monk named Vasubandhu. She also spent the year before her death from cancer at age fifty-one completing a book about feminist spirituality and feminist philosophy. She wrote the book in Calgary in 1994–95 while taking her first sabbatical leave from the University of Alberta. She was also battling lung cancer at the time, and that experience served to open her eyes to different ways of looking at life and death. "The joy of seeing oneself with new eyes after being released from unfocused fear, anger and sadness, allows the spirit to sing," she wrote in her posthumously published book, *Bodied Mindfulness: Women's Spirits, Bodies and Places.*

Her posthumous writing shows that Tomm's final journey was one of acceptance and living joyfully in the moment. She knew she was dying, and she knew what the disease was doing to her body. Being freed from the need to cure her disease, she was able to focus her energy on healing in the spiritual sense, and ultimately to share a final consummation with those who loved her. "It never occurred to her to give in to the disease and give up on her wonderful life," wrote her academic colleague Gerry Dyer, also a wife and mother, in a memorial tribute. "She appeared to be stronger than the rest of us when it should have been the other way round."

Sandra Botting
Pioneering midwife

1947–1999

The practice of midwifery has a long and distinguished history in Europe, but in Canada, until the 1990s, it had great difficulty gaining legal recognition. The natural process of childbirth was viewed by some members of the medical profession as being almost like a health problem, best treated by a physician, preferably in a hospital.

The change, when it happened, occurred because of the determination of Sandra Botting, a radiology technologist from Saskatoon who came to Calgary in the mid-1960s. She became involved in the midwifery movement after two difficult births during her first marriage.

In 1969, Botting had her first child, in a hospital, and she suffered through all the procedures she would later come to deplore. It was a forceps delivery that left her drugged, with legs strapped in stirrups, and a "terrible empty feeling of separation from the baby and the rest of my family." She would later refer to it as a "rape" and an "extraction." There was so much pain afterward that she "couldn't sit down for a week."

The second time she gave birth, two years later, was similarly harrowing. "My husband was outside pacing, my little girl was at home separated from us, and I was alone in a room, sore." She was knocked out with medication and subsequently suffered postpartum depression.

After that, her marriage fell apart. She moved in with Ron Botting, a close friend of five years. She began to read books about midwifery, including information on its history and the politics that led to it being discredited in North America during the early part of the twentieth century.

In 1974, Sandra was pregnant for the third time. With husband Ron and several friends supporting her, she began making preparations for a home birth. They couldn't find an available doctor or midwife to attend, so they studied obstetrical texts and did it themselves, with a video camera there to record the event. That birth marked the beginning of Sandra's involvement in the alternative childbirth movement. She founded the Alternative Birthing Group of Calgary, now called Birth Unlimited, and served as its first president. She began attending home births with Una Jean Underwood, an American-born Calgary physician, and took correspondence courses in midwifery.

Her fourth birth, in 1977, was a quiet, calm delivery with no fear or trauma. "The ultimate experience," she called it. By that time, Sandra was becoming a powerful voice for midwifery, serving as president of the Midwives' Alliance of North America, practising midwifery, risking prosecution, and lobbying for legal status for midwives in Canada—by then the only western industrialized nation where midwifery was still illegal. "Do you know what kind of company we're in?" Sandra asked a reporter. "El Salvador, Dominican Republic, New Guinea, Burundi—and then there's Canada. We stick out like a sore thumb."

In 1981, the Alberta College of Physicians and Surgeons prohibited doctors from attending home births. A college official said, "We don't care if these women choose to have their babies on top of a manure pile as long as they leave the medical profession out of their bad decisions." Because of this hostility, Sandra's physician friend Una Jean Underwood returned to the United States, leaving Sandra uncertain as to what to do next.

The college's ruling drove the home-birth movement underground for several years. Sandra continued to press for legal recognition of midwifery as a licensed profession under Alberta's Health Disciplines Act. Operating outside the law—though never prosecuted—she helped deliver more than five hundred babies, mostly in the early morning hours, sometimes after driving through blizzards to rural locations.

In 1992, the tide started turning. The provincial government announced that Alberta would become the second province after Ontario to legalize midwifery. Sandra joined the government committee appointed to establish rules for the profession, working to ensure that the model of midwifery in Alberta would meet the needs of families and professionals.

Alberta's midwifery bill finally became law in 1995. "I did wonder if I would actually live to see it," said Sandra. She only lived another four years. In February 1999 she was diagnosed with cancer at age fifty-one, and she died three months later. Three days before her death, on the International Day of the Midwife, she was recognized in the Alberta legislature for her dedication to the profession of midwifery. Her life, in the words of a friend, had been "testimony to the importance of finding purpose, pursuing it fiercely, and blazing new trails along the way."

Although a big battle was won when Alberta's midwives received legal recognition, the war was far from over. In early 2001, an increase in malpractice insurance premiums from four thousand dollars to fifteen thousand dollars a year threatened to put many of them out of business. An appeal to the provincial government for financial assistance resulted in a one-time grant from Alberta Health, in April 2001, to cover the increased premiums. However, the midwives said the crisis would only be fully averted when the province agreed to pay for midwives' fees.

Irma Parhad

Medical researcher

1948–1994

The Alberta Heritage Foundation for Medical Research was established by the provincial government in 1980 with a three-hundred-
million-dollar endowment. Within a few years it had turned both the
University of Alberta and the University of Calgary into major cen-
tres of medical research, earning international acclaim for their discoveries and attracting some of the top medical investigators from
around the world.

Irma Parhad was one of the more than five thousand researchers
who applied for foundation scholarships during the first five years of
the government program. She was one of the fewer than two hundred whose applications were successful. She was a neurologist with
a special interest in aging nerve cells, and during her ten years in
Calgary she made major contributions to understanding the causes
of degenerative brain diseases.

She was born in Iraq and as a small child revealed something of
the stubbornness and determination that would define her life and
career. It came during an exchange with her father, a neurosurgeon
who challenged his six children to read, compose essays, solve problems, and generally excel. Displeased with something she had done,
he told young Irma that she should obey him or leave the house. She
responded by going out into the garden and sitting there until her
father relented. That obstinacy shaped the rest of her life.

As her father had wished, she excelled in school. After attending
French-language convent schools in Baghdad, and learning several
languages including English and German, she left at age eighteen
for college in the United States. She graduated from Chicago's
Loyola School of Medicine in 1973, and then began a residency in
neurology in Albany, New York. She had, by that time, decided on
a career in research. After completing her neurology residency,

she trained in neuropathology and neurovirology at the University of Pittsburgh and the University of California in San Francisco.

In 1978, Irma married Arthur Clark, a fellow medical professional. They moved to Baltimore, Maryland, where Irma joined the prestigious medicine faculty at Johns Hopkins University. After six years there, Irma received the foundation grant that allowed her to establish her research program at the University of Calgary, probing the causes of Alzheimer's disease and related degenerative disorders of the nervous system.

As well as doing research, Irma also worked as a clinician, seeing patients with degenerative brain diseases. She was also founder and director of the university's Dementia Research Clinic, providing a setting for therapeutic trials and other clinical studies. "She was compulsively attentive to details both in the clinic and in the laboratory," noted her husband.

Her research work steadily flowered. One of her laboratory's more startling discoveries was that, contrary to long-held scientific belief, human nerve cells damaged by Gehrig's disease might be able to repair themselves. Her lab also made major contributions toward understanding the molecular basis of aging in the brain. The breakthroughs seemed to be inspired by Irma's philosophy that "problems are there to be solved." As her husband observed, "The first step in her undertakings was the decisive one, the point at which she set her mind on some objective. Then the stubbornness took over and she drove doggedly against the elements of adversity to reach her destination."

Her work brought her national and international recognition. In 1989, she became a Medical Research Council of Canada scientist, and in 1992, she was appointed professor of pathology and clinical neurosciences at the University of Calgary.

During this same period, she saw her country of origin destroyed by the Gulf War. While prudence might have dictated that a person of Iraqi birth remain silent, she could not hide the sorrow and outrage she felt as she watched the devastation of the country where she had grown up. She described the experience as a turning point in her life.

In 1992, Irma became a Canadian citizen. She had grown to love

Calgary and the nearby Rocky Mountains, where she hiked and skied with the same spirit of determination that she brought to her professional work. Just weeks before she was diagnosed with cancer, she completed a three-hundred-kilometre mountain bike trip. For gentler recreation she liked to garden, read, and listen to friends reading aloud from Marquez, Nabokov, or Proust.

Her life seemed to overflow with plans and new undertakings. Learning of an increase in life expectancy among Canadians, she enthused, "We're all going to live to be ninety."

For Irma, however, it was to be another story. In June 1993, when she was forty-five, she learned that she had cancer and was told she had less than two years to live.

She fought her illness with characteristic determination. She managed to ski again after two major surgeries and several courses of chemotherapy. She continued to cultivate her garden of rocks and evergreens, had a cabin renovated, and had new shelves and cabinets built in her home. "The defiant spirit and irrepressible enthusiasm for living stayed with her until her ability to express it was extinguished in the last few days of her life," said her husband.

Yet, inevitably, the defiance and the enthusiasm were accompanied by a deep sense of regret and loss. She talked wistfully about the time a family of hoary marmots gathered at her feet while she was hiking and remarked sadly that she would never see their likes again. She died in June 1994 at age forty-six. Her estate continues to fund various worthy causes including an annual lecture series addressing factors that influence the health and welfare of people around the world.

Nelson Small Legs, Jr.

Native activist

1953–1976

On 19 May 1976, a twenty-three-year-old Native activist named Nelson Small Legs, Jr., dressed himself in traditional Peigan costume, lay down on his bed, and shot himself through the heart with a rifle. His suicide note made front-page headlines across Canada. "I give up my life in protest to the present conditions concerning Indian people of southern Alberta. I also give my life in the hopes of a full-scale investigation into the dept. of Indian Affairs corruption. For one hundred years Indians have suffered. Must they suffer another one hundred years? My suicide should open the eyes of non-Indians into how much we've suffered."

Journalists, sociologists, and psychologists converged on the Small Legs home at Brocket, west of Lethbridge, hoping to uncover reasons for the suicide. Nearly all came away without answers. Nothing in his background suggested that his life might end one day in such a violent and public way. In fact, Small Legs seemed to be a well-adjusted young man, married with two young daughters, who had sampled the excesses of white Canadian society and rejected them to live by the tenets of his Peigan heritage.

Small Legs was raised in a log home on the Peigan reserve during a time when the horse and buggy was still used on the reserve for private transportation, and the train was the main means of public transport. Small Legs—whose family called him Coco—attended Roman Catholic mission day schools and boarding schools on the reserve until he was thirteen. With his younger brother, Devalon, he left the reserve in 1966 as part of a government program to assimilate Natives into the public education system, and he moved into Lethbridge where he lived in white foster homes while attending school.

At age fourteen, Small Legs became the first Native to join the Lethbridge Squadron Air Cadets of Canada. A fine athlete, he played football throughout the years he attended Catholic Central High School in Lethbridge, and he was in line for a university football scholarship until he was expelled from Lethbridge Community College. The college claimed he was expelled for lack of attendance. Small Legs said it was a result of a threat from the Department of Indian Affairs to cut off his tuition funding after he took part in a November 1974 sit in at the federal Indian Affairs office in Calgary.

Before attending Lethbridge Community College, Small Legs had gone through a rough couple of years, drinking heavily and taking hard drugs. The legal drinking age in Alberta had dropped from twenty-one to eighteen, liquor had become available on reserves, and "that spelled the ruin of our people from that day forward," said Devalon. The brothers managed to escape from the drinking and drug scene, sobered up, and returned to the reserve where they spent time with tribal elders, medicine men, and spiritual leaders. They learned how to live the Native way of life, participating in sweat lodge purification ceremonies, smoking sweetgrass, and healing themselves physically and emotionally. They learned from the elders, said Devalon, "that once you pick up the pipe to use as the instrument of prayer, you do not pick it up for yourself, you pick it up for all mankind."

As his understanding of Native culture grew, Nelson looked for ways to save other Natives from the kind of alcohol and drug abuse with which he had been involved. He was one of the founders of the Alberta chapter of the American Indian Movement (AIM), and he worked the streets of Fort Macleod, Pincher Creek, Lethbridge, and Cardston, taking intoxicated reserve residents to their homes before police could pick them up.

The RCMP and federal Indian Affairs officials viewed the American Indian Movement as a threat to Canada's national security because of its militant activities in the United States. Because the AIM members called themselves "warriors," they were often characterized in the media—incorrectly, as it turned out—as a group of gun-toting Natives spoiling for a fight. As far as Canadian government officials were concerned, AIM Canada was nothing more than an imported version of the American movement, and its goal was anarchy. This view of the movement resulted in various clashes between the RCMP and Canadian AIM members, starting with a 1973 stand-off in Cache Creek, British Columbia, when a group of Stuctwesemc band activists blockaded the Cariboo Highway to protest poor housing conditions on the Bonaparte reserve.

However, as far as Nelson Small Legs was concerned, peaceful civic demonstrations, not violent confrontations, were the way to draw attention to Native problems in Canada. AIM Canada was loosely aligned with the hard-line militants in the United States who occupied the South Dakota reservation hamlet of Wounded Knee by force in 1973. However, the goal of the Canadian movement was to improve the status of Natives through legal and peaceful means. There was no conspiracy, no intent to hurt or wound, and no situation where the Canadian AIM members carried arms. Small Legs believed the future belonged to Natives bearing university degrees, not rifles. "The AIM ideology is not at odds with the goals of Canadian society in general," wrote Calgary anthropologist Joan Ryan in her book, *Wall of Words: The Betrayal of the Urban Indian.* "The most 'violent' comment made by any of the men is that they would lay down their own lives if they had to do so."

Small Legs first became involved in civic protest in 1974, when it seemed clear to him that the Calgary Urban Treaty Indian Alliance (CUTIA) was being frustrated in its efforts to provide alternative social services to status Indians living in Calgary. CUTIA had been established in 1972 to serve the needs of Natives migrating from the reserves to the city, but requests to the federal government for sustained funding were unheard. Some CUTIA workers were forced to go on welfare because their wages were not being paid. Others returned to the reserves and found short-lived jobs with the soon-to-be-abolished Company of Young Canadians program, a federal community development initiative which itself was undergoing a funding crisis at that time.

In August 1974, Small Legs took part in a short sit-in at the Indian Affairs office in Calgary. This resulted in a promise from then Indian Affairs minister Jean Chrétien to have the requested funding authorized immediately. Three months later, with funds still not forthcoming, CUTIA workers—assisted by members of AIM Canada—staged an all-day sit-in at the Indian Affairs office. This resulted in public mischief charges being laid against CUTIA director Roy Little Chief and AIM Canada national director Ed Burnstick.

In July 1975, AIM and CUTIA threatened to disrupt the Calgary Stampede to draw public attention to the plight of urban Natives, and at the same time, to comment on what they perceived as the abuse of Natives by the Stampede board. This planned action was diverted when the Stampede board agreed to listen to allegations that the Natives comprised little more than "an extension to the midway" and were not included as equals in the planning for the Stampede.

In October 1975, Small Legs and a group of Native chiefs met in Calgary with Indian Affairs representatives to discuss the various problems facing urbanized Natives in the Calgary area. The meeting ended when the government offered to finance a fifty-thousand-dollar study of the situation. However, the study never took place, and CUTIA continued to be thwarted in its efforts to get government funding for its programs.

In May 1976, the Berger Commission hearings into the proposed construction of a pipeline to transport natural gas and oil from the Arctic Ocean to Alberta were held in Calgary. These hearings were not directly related to CUTIA's efforts, but because they dealt with Native land claims and aboriginal rights, they were of great interest to Small Legs. He attended the hearings and made an impassioned presentation in which he talked about Native children melting down vinyl LP records for their alcohol content.

"This is truth, this is basic grassroots truth. This is what the dominant society has done to Native people all across Canada," said Small Legs. "And if they go through that change of values in the Northwest Territories, I see the same corruption. Booze, alcohol!"

Two days later, Small Legs took his own life. The funeral was shown on national television, and viewers across Canada witnessed an unforgettable image when Nelson Small Legs, Jr.'s horse, riderless but fully saddled, was led by Nelson's brother to the cemetery. Prime Minister Trudeau promised, in Parliament, to investigate the death and the issues raised in Nelson's suicide note, but the investigation never took place.

Nelson's father, Nelson Small Legs, Sr., who had been quietly active in Peigan politics as a social worker and band councillor, was inspired by his son's words to become more highly visible. "Someone must take the first step to show the conditions Indians live in," the younger Nelson had written in his suicide note. The first step for the elder Nelson was to become elected chief of the Peigan reserve and to start working for the things—better housing, education, jobs—that had been important to his son.

Two years after his son died, the elder Nelson organized a blockade to stop district waterworks employees from crossing the reserve to open an irrigation weir on the Oldman River, near where the younger Nelson is buried. The elder Nelson alleged that the provincial government had illegally seized 4.1 acres of unsurrendered reserve land to build the weir, and he refused the province permission to open the canal gates and flood farmland. The authorities responded by moving in with an army helicopter and eighty RCMP officers in riot gear. Nelson, Sr., agreed only to lift the blockade when the province agreed to pay the Peigans $3.5 million for the 4.1 acres. He noted, however, that there was no compensation for either the Crowsnest Pass highway or the railway line that sliced through the reserve.

Because Small Legs, Sr., defied the authorities with his 1978 blockade, he earned a reputation for militancy that echoed in the 1990 posturing of Peigan activist Milton Born With a Tooth, who made headlines when he fired rifle shots in the air to warn the government against using the flood waters of the massive new Oldman River dam to destroy the sacred burial grounds and ceremonial sites of the Peigans. Small Legs, Sr., agreed with the sentiment, but he disagreed with the guerrilla tactic of using firearms to make a point. Change should be effected through negotiations, he said. He felt Peigans should place their faith in their Creator and try to see previous injustices against them as "passing ignorance."

A dozen years after his son's death, Small Legs, Sr., said sadly that conditions for young Natives had not improved. His son had given his life to bring attention to something he felt was important, but no change for the better had taken place. Some young Natives were turning to the elders for advice, but more were turning to alcohol and drugs. "Most want work, but there's no money to create jobs," said Nelson Small Legs, Sr., He died in 1993 at age sixty-one.

Afterword

I am indebted to the following authors for doing the spadework that made it possible for me to write *Alberta Originals: Stories of Albertans Who Made a Difference*:

Ken Bolton, Sharon A. Fogarty, Donaleen Saul, and Sheonaid Ursan for *The Albertans*; Annora Brown for *Sketches from Life*; Hugh A. Dempsey for *Calgary: Spirit of the West*; David R. Elliott and Iris Miller for *Bible Bill: A Biography of William Aberhart*; Bruno Engler and R. W. Sandford for *A Mountain Life: The Stories and Photographs of Bruno Engler*; Max Foran and Sheilagh S. Jameson for *Citymakers: Calgarians after the Frontier*; Peter Foster for *The Blue-Eyed Sheiks: The Canadian Oil Establishment*; John F. Gilpin for *Edmonton: Gateway to the North*; James H. Gray for *From a Brand of its Own: The 100-year History of the Calgary Exhibition and Stampede;* Harald Gunderson for *The Linder Legend: The Story of ProRodeo and its Champion*; The Historical Society of Alberta for *William Stewart Herron: Father of the Petroleum Industry in Alberta;* Monica Hopkins for *Letters from a Lady Rancher*; Lillian Knupp for *Twigs of the Medicine Tree Country*; Nancy Langford for *Politics, Pitchforks and Pickle Jars: 75 Years of Organized Farm Women in Alberta*; Daniel S. Levy for *Two-Gun Cohen: A Biography*; Grant MacEwan for *Pat Burns: Cattle King, The Sodbusters, Frederick Haultain: Frontier Statesman of the Canadian Northwest,* and *Fifty Mighty Men*; J. G. MacGregor for *Edmonton: A History*; Peter McKenzie-Brown and Stacey Phillips for *In Balance: An Account of Alberta's CA Profession, 1910–2000*; Nancy Millar for *The Famous Five: Emily Murphy and the Case of the Missing Persons*; Ruth Oltmann for *Lizzie Rummel: Baroness of the Canadian Rockies*; Beverly Matson Rasporich and Christine Mason Sutherland for *Woman as Artist: Papers in Honour of Marsha Hanen*; Kay Sanderson for *200 Remarkable Alberta Women;* Mary Clark Sheppard for *Oil Sands Scientist: The Letters of Karl A. Clark, 1920–1949*; Diane King Stuemer for *Hawrelak: The Story*; Winnie Tomm for *Bodied Mindfulness: Women's Spirits, Bodies and Places*; Paul Voisey for *A Preacher's Frontier: The Castor, Alberta Letters of Rev. Martin W. Holdom, 1909–12*; Jon Whyte for *Mountain*

Glory: The Art of Peter and Catharine Whyte; and Gary W. Zeman for *Alberta on Ice.*

Index

About the Author

Brian Brennan is a Dublin-born writer and musician who immigrated to Canada in 1966 and has lived and worked in Calgary since 1974. His recent books include *Building a Province: 60 Alberta Lives*, published by Fifth House Ltd. in 2000, and *Máire Bhuí Ní Laoire: A Poet of her People*, a literary biography of an Irish folk poet published in Ireland by The Collins Press. He is also the co-author and co-editor of *Deadlines & Diversity: Journalism Ethics in a Changing World*, published by Fernwood in 1996.

Web site: http://www.brian-brennan.com